# MND The Club You Don't Want To Join

A Young Man's Journey Navigating Terminal Illness, Disability and Independence

Samuel Hayden-Harler

ISBN: 9798299435498 (Paperback)

Book cover by Ryan Mulford.

Book design by Ryan Mulford.

# Contents

I dedicate this book to those living with life-limiting illnesses and those who love and care for them.

I also dedicate this to the many MND Warriors who we have sadly lost, and who paved the way for others like me. I am inspired by their strength, courage and determination.

# Acknowledgements

Firstly, a huge thank you to my family for everything you do every day in keeping me going. I know it is not easy and the journey so far has had many highs and lows. Your unwavering support and care means so much to me, as we navigate the unknown. I know life has thrown a huge curve ball our way and we try our best to get through each day, and that is all that we can do. You have kept me going on the days when I thought I couldn't. I will never forget all that you have done.

Thanks to my dear friends, without whom and without which, I don't know where I'd be. We've laughed, cried and everything else in between. We've seen each other go through life, cheering the many achievements and celebrations, and lent a listening ear during harder times. Our friendship has stood the test of time and I'm forever thankful that we've had the time that we had. Although our lives have changed over the years, we embraced every moment and you being my chosen family means more than you'll know.

I'd like to thank the Motor Neurone Disease Association for supporting me throughout my MND journey and for providing me with many opportunities and ways in which to share my story. In particular thanks to Esther, Emily and Dominique for all the chats, projects and campaigns you let me be a part of.

Dr Ellis, Dr Ramsay and my entire care team: I appreciate your time, guidance, knowledge and patience. This has been the toughest experience for me to live through, a journey with many unknowns and challenges to overcome.

To Adeep, Dani, Kirsty, Martha and Vishnu. You have become family and anyone who can take me from barely awake to fully buffed and polished, deserves a medal!

My son who made it possible for me to be a Dad, which has equally been the best and most exhausting job in the world! I hope you're as proud of me as I am of you.

Finally, thank YOU for buying my book! It was always a distant dream to publish a book one day and for that to be my legacy. I am so very thankful that you have chosen to read my story and to make my dream a reality.

As you will read, this is my experience of living with MND. It's an honest and emotional account of my life. I do not sugar-coat things, and I discuss topics that may upset or provoke you. I will also be introducing you to others who have kindly share their experiences.

Much love,

Sam x

# Foreword

Life – it is a small word with huge gravitas; a complex concept which throws many difficult existential questions our way; "what is my purpose on this Earth?" "What is the meaning of life?" "And just how heaped should a 'heaped teaspoon' *really* be...?"

Let's be abundantly clear, Motor Neurone Disease is a cruel, relentless and agnostic condition that doesn't give a damn who you are or what plans you've made for the future. However, this book is honest, vulnerable, shocking, heartwarming and funny. Yes, that's right – it is also funny. It takes a certain type of dark humour to poke fun at your own terminal illness and that is why this book delivers on so many levels *[insert joke here about Sam not being able to take the stairs]*.

This book will also show how, even in 2025, society is not designed for those with a disability, and is still not fully accepting of individuals considered outside of the 'norm'. So much more needs to be done to ensure everyone is seen, embraced and looked after in this world – I guarantee at the end of this book you'll be better informed, deeply moved and hopefully even angered enough to help make a difference.

This book also talks openly about the opposite of life – you know, the "d-word"... that many of us avoid talking about: but fear not, there are 15 chapters to read first before you get to that bit. Until then, try and wrap your head around the fact that Sam wrote this book using just his face... yes, his *face*... my face can't even disguise boredom properly, let alone write a bloody book.

Sam, along with so many MND warriors before him, alongside him and succeeding him have proven, are proving and will continue to prove that, even though the body is changing, failing – or whatever you want to call it – the brain, spirit, wit and raw self are still intact. Therefore, what you're about to read isn't just a medical memoir or an emotional 'woe is me' sob story – it is a love letter to resilience, a middle finger to despair and an open invitation to understand MND – from someone who knows it far too well.

So, dear reader, enjoy!

*(That is not a request; that is an order)*

Love,

ClairexXx

P.S. Thank you Sam from the bottom of my heart for asking me to write this foreword; it is an honor.

# Introduction

"I'D HATE TO BE *diagnosed with a terminal illness.*"

This thought had unexpectedly crossed my mind at times in my life, along with millions of others across the world, I'm sure. The truth is that very few will experience the crippling anxiety-inducing pain that such a diagnosis brings. However, many like me are expected to live through the stupidly long unnecessary waiting times, to be met with the words you never think you'll ever have to hear, unless they feature in a nightmare. That same nightmare is sadly the stark reality for some.

In summer 2024, I was in Blackpool ticking off a bucket list moment – more about that later on. It was a beautiful sunny day and I was sat in my wheelchair at the end of the pier on my own, next to a family openly discussing old age. Not one to purposely eavesdrop, as I glanced out to sea, I nonetheless began tuning into their conversation with interest as they conversed about life-changing illnesses. They mentioned that some family members had been diagnosed with life-limiting illnesses and the young daughter said they wouldn't know how to deal with such news. I listened with interest as I had been living with Motor Neurone Disease (MND) after being diagnosed on

Saturday 5th March 2022. I empathised with them, but had to remind myself that I was living proof of that scenario.

I was just 35 years old when I was diagnosed. I naively thought this was an illness only seen in older generations. How wrong I was. Even the current guidance provided by the NHS states that the illness is mainly diagnosed in those aged 50 and above, but that there are individuals diagnosed younger, in their 40s. I am part of a sadly ever-growing community of warriors diagnosed in their 20s and 30s. We find ourselves joining 'The membership club nobody wants to join'.

I am one of approximately 5,000 people in the UK living with this life-limiting illness that is likely to kill most within two to five years. Despite being labelled as a "rare illness", one in 300 are diagnosed. I do not consider those odds to be rare at all. I consider it highly likely that most families will be affected by MND at some point in their lifetime. However so little is known about what causes it.

The illness is misunderstood by many; it is often mistaken for other illnesses such as MS. As very few are truly exposed to it, assumptions are often made and this is a key reason why I am so passionate about raising awareness.

So what is MND? It is also referred to Amyotrophic Lateral Sclerosis (ALS), a neurological disease that results in the nerves from the brain to the body being damaged and broken, for reasons which remain unknown. Over time, this causes muscle wastage throughout the entire body, meaning it is paralysed. Muscle and limb function reduce, and eventually the entire body stops functioning.

Research to find a cure for MND continues, with many advances having been made over the last few decades. This vital research can only happen due to there being funds available, which is why raising awareness to help fundraise is necessary. You may remember the 'ALS Ice Bucket Challenge' which went viral in 2014, which involved a bucket of ice water being poured over someone's head in return for a donation to the ALS or MND Association. According to Wikipedia, it raised more than $220m worldwide.

Technology has come a long way, and it enables me to have a quality of life. I now use my iPhone and MacBook entirely hands-free. I proudly write this book using the head control functionality, typing on the on-screen keyboard using facial expressions such as smiling, scrunching my nose and raising my eyebrows to perform particular tasks. I also have the ability to use dictation software. I'll explain more about how this all works later on. It is a time-consuming process, but it still enables me to get the job done. As you'll discover, I focus on what I can do, not what I can't. I achieve the same outcome as those who are able-bodied, but I do it differently. It saddens me to know that, before this technology existed, I would simply have been unable to do much, let alone communicate. I have become fiercely independent because of MND.

The reasons and inspiration for writing this book and sharing my story are varied. It's said that each of us writes our own unique story and so this is my book, from me to you. This is not the story, nor the ending I ever envisaged I would write, but alas it is mine nonetheless. It has allowed me to reflect on my life in many ways. Yes, my life will be much shorter than I expected it to be and I will miss many life events, but I consider that I have lived a lot in my time. I am often expected to be bitter and angry about my illness but I can truthfully say that I am not. I don't have the time or energy to hold onto negative feelings. I want to get on with my life and to leave a positive legacy. I wanted to create something that did not exist when I was searching for others going through the same pre- and post-diagnostic process. I still struggle to see others like me, and I hope my legacy is that this book helps and supports others in their understanding of MND, life-limiting illnesses and the realities of living with them.

Someone once said to me, "You can't add time to life, but you can add life to time," and I firmly believe that I have done that. While it is indeed a scary path to travel, there are, believe it or not, beautiful moments that have come from it too.

If I was given £1 for every time I heard someone say, "That's what Stephen Hawking had; he lived for decades. You'll be fine", I would be filthy rich. It is true that he did live for many decades with MND, but it is extremely rare to live for multiple decades. There are many misconceptions surrounding the illnesses that I will try to address in this book. Despite its "rare" label, very little is known about it, which means there is currently no cure, only treatments, which are there to manage symptoms. There is a lack of government funding to support the cost of research and medical trials. It is mainly down to those affected by MND to raise funds.

A significant part of this is thanks to fellow warriors and former rugby players Rob Burrow, Doddie Weir, and Ed Slater and the former football player Marcus Stewart, who have raised huge amounts and raised the profile of MND. Kevin Sinfield OBE is a huge supporter of the MND community and has raised millions, which is going to support vital research, treatments, and those living with MND.

Every person with MND follows a different trajectory and is highly unlikely to follow the same journey as a fellow warrior. MND is not an illness that presents the same symptoms for each person. Many medical professionals involved in my care and support have told me that everyone will have different symptoms. Some may have full limb function, whereas others have limited or no use at all. There are others who have no voice, but some who never lose it. There will be some who encounter breathing or swallowing difficulties and, again, those who don't. This makes it a complex illness is a reason why still so little is known about it. I am personally aware of warriors who have died within six months of diagnosis, and others who lived for more than a decade. There are medical staff who will never be involved with an MND patient which is why education and awareness is imperative. The only thing we can do is to cling onto hope that medical advances happen in our lifetime.

# Chapter 1: Newly diagnosed?

Firstly, you're going to be OK. You are so much stronger than you believe you are.

There will be so much to get your head around but, above all else, be kind to yourself. Allow yourself to be in all of your emotions. It may take time to even contemplate trying to understand what you have been told. It's not only life-changing, but it also alters your perspective on pretty much your entire life. Find and surround yourself with people who will uplift and support you. If that means letting go of some people and relationships, that's OK. You have to focus on you and what matters to you.

Look for a small pocket of happiness in every day. It doesn't have to be anything extravagant or costly. It could be feeling the sun on your skin, a phone call with a friend or listening to your favourite song. You may have days when it'll all feel too much and overwhelming; it'll be those slices of happiness that see you through the tougher times. Lean on people who will give you strength. Remember, you are absolutely allowed to laugh and have fun. As much as I was sad, humour and laughter were, and still are, coping mechanisms for me. I let others inject dry or dark humour at my illness, but be aware that not everyone will share the same outlook. Every person diagnosed will journey their own path and so we will have similar, but not identical experiences.

Filter what you choose to read about MND. There are thousands of pieces of content sharing misinformation or statistics that are simply not trustworthy. Navigate to reliable sources such as the MNDA (or the equivalent in your country) to ensure that what you are absorbing is factual. There are multiple MND charities in the UK and worldwide that provide guidance and support, and that can assist you in the weeks, months and years ahead. They have many services available that can signpost you to any entitlement or funding available, and discuss them with you.

If you're able to and feel comfortable to do so, locate others in a similar position across social platforms who are part of the wider MND community. There's an unspoken understanding and you'll be welcomed without question. Personally, I found that embracing a positive mindset and outlook really helped me in approaching every day. I still have grey days but, as I now know, they soon pass. It's also understandable that this may not be how you choose to live.

As you'll read, this is my experience of living with MND. I've surrounded myself with people who champion my cause and who have kept my spirits high. Every person I have met living with MND has had their individual experience.

I do not "suffer with" or "suffer from" MND. I live with it, almost like an uninvited and unwelcome visitor.

**If you're undergoing testing...**

Much like the above, you're going through a process that carries with it lots of questions. You may not have answers to these questions for some time, so try to find something that will help distract you. I would refrain from self-diagnosing – allow the medical professionals to do what they need to do. I often receive messages from others who are in the midst of testing and who reach out for guidance. I will help when I can (and remember, not everyone will want to) but please be mindful of people who have been diagnosed.

I would always recommend reliable sources of information and speaking with the appropriate helplines that can guide you.

# Chapter 2: Losing Grip

My work as an Insurance Claims Technician was firmly placed on hold in June 2020, as I was about to finish and embark on a period of adoption leave for a year, as our son was coming home around this time. I was super excited to be leaving full-time employment as I was about to become a dad after almost two years of the adoption approval process. Our boy, who we will refer to as "M" or Little Man to protect his identity, was officially going to make our family grow. Thanks to the Covid-19 pandemic and multiple lock-downs, my husband James and I faced long delays as the family courts struggled with the sheer number of cases while they were adhering to government guidelines and social distancing.

Becoming fathers overnight, despite having prepared for all eventualities, was still quite a shock. We all had to forge a new routine and slowly adapt to our new life as parents. We had received specific training from our adoption agency, but nothing could really prepare us for what lay ahead. To allow for a smooth transition from his foster carers to his forever home, our introduction period and hand-over lasted several weeks, as we started to take on some responsibilities from his amazing foster carers. They had been preparing him for the life-changing transition that was about to take place. Several days into the transition I suddenly became overwhelmed with crippling anxiety and fear. Was I good enough to be his father? Would he like us? I couldn't stop the conflicting emotions as we were embarking on what we had dreamt of, but I was equally petrified. I eventually called our social worker as I sat on the foster carer's kitchen floor, in tears, hidden away from view.

"*Sam, what you're feeling is entirely normal, just like any new relationship, feelings grow in time. As long as you like him, you're off to a good start*". This comforted me; maybe I had been too harsh on myself and was expecting too much too soon. The rest of the introductions went well although I tried to hide my anxiety. We were soon ready to start life as a new family. I still recall M as he walked into his forever home and saw the huge array of toys ready for him to play with. His foster carer was with us for the end of the transition, ensuring there was a smooth hand-over. The first night was tough for us all. A new bed, bedroom and belongings, which must have been so scary for him. He cried as he got into bed, his foster carer calmed and reassured him as he drifted off to sleep. We sat downstairs in the lounge, fixated on the video monitor as we carefully watched his every move. The first few days were spent playing, fuelled by caffeine and adrenaline. The days and nights soon turned into weeks and months. We had a lovely summer, enjoying days out, visits from family and friends and building a bond as a new family.

We were looking forward to our first Christmas together when I started to notice that unscrewing lids and bottle tops felt troublesome; I really had to squeeze my right hand tightly to unscrew one. I had experienced the odd difficulty before, but that was for lids that were impossible to open – this felt different. Some I could open, some I couldn't. I really had to focus, and it began to feel like I had somehow lost strength. I thought nothing of it and instead focussed my attention on our first family Christmas. I thought that maybe I was rundown in energy from becoming a new parent.

By now, M was going to nursery and forest school, an outdoor educational setting that encourages learning via multiple activities such as camp fires. This meant that, for three days a week he was busy and on those days I would get chores completed and have some time for myself. I had been away from work for almost eight months by this time, and I made the decision to return to work part-time. My hand hadn't shown any further issues since I first noticed the slight weakness, but after I had been back at work for a few months I noticed an increasing discomfort in my right wrist. Some days it was there, and others it wasn't. It got to the point that I couldn't ignore my hand and wrist any longer. I bought wrist supports, as I suspected the long break away from typing on a keyboard may be causing a repetitive strain injury. Weeks went by and the loss of strength had become a little more noticeable now and it didn't feel that this was going to correct itself.

I'm not one for visiting the doctor, but I hastily made the call to my GP and booked an appointment for a few days' time to see a nurse. At this stage I noticed that I had lost muscle around the base of my right thumb – which was worrying – but I wanted to see what they thought. Maybe I was overreacting to something trivial. My right knee and leg also felt different, it didn't feel as supportive as my left. The nurse checked my reflexes and examined my arms and legs and the small muscle loss before explaining, "*Neurologically, you're fine*". That gave me the confidence and reassurance to know it was nothing sinister. The nurse wanted to send me for a physiotherapy assessment to see if that would help. The referral was made but, as the pandemic had caused delays, it was three months before my appointment. I carried on with life and paid no more attention to it.

The day of my assessment came; while I was a little anxious and apprehensive, I wasn't worried as the nurse had said I was fine. I was called in and underwent my physical examination. She noticed that my right wrist was weaker than the left, but she couldn't tell why. I was given a small hand weight to try a lift but had difficulty in doing so, while trying to keep my arm flat on the table. She said that, as her senior colleague was in the same building, she wanted him to examine me. I mentioned my leg, but as my GP hadn't specifically requested this, they said they would need to refer me separately for this, which was annoying. A few moments later, her colleague joined us and carried out a similar examination before asking me if I could whistle, which I did. I was also asked to walk on my tiptoes which I completed with ease. I found these requests somewhat strange but trusted that there was a method to the madness. He kept quiet before I asked what he thought it was. He said that he wanted to send me for tests along with a referral to an NHS Neurologist. "What is it?" I asked frantically. "I don't know" he said. "I don't think this is muscle related, I think this may be neurological".

Holy fuck. Had I heard him properly? This was now a little more sinister. I had already been told I was fine neurologically, but now that didn't appear to be the case. It was not the response I had expected to hear, but there wasn't much I could do. The clinician wouldn't say any more, which further added to my growing anxiety. For now it was a waiting game, as we needed the referrals for blood tests, an MRI and a nerve conduction study.

While waiting for the second referral and appointment, the blood test was returned; it was inconclusive and showed nothing of concern. A month later, I was sat in the hospital waiting room, waiting to be called for my MRI scan. I had been asked to complete a form beforehand. I noticed that holding and writing with a pen not only required my focussed attention but that my handwriting was messier than normal. I knew I didn't have the best handwriting but could this be linked to the symptoms that had presented? I still thought I had repetitive strain injury. I was called in for the scan and was prepared before popping myself onto the machine. "The scan will last about forty-five minutes and you must remain completely still".

"OK" I muttered, but my inner voice questioned how I was going to lie still for that long. Somehow I managed to do it, just by closing my eyes and trying to quiet my mind. I let my mind go to a nicer place and before long the scan was over. I returned home and carried on with life for a few weeks before receiving a letter inviting me to King's College Hospital on New Year's Eve for a nerve conduction study. That'll be a New Year's I won't forget!

Nerve conduction sounded like an ancient torture practice or something used in a concentration camp to inflict pain. My mind got the better of me and most days I would search Google, listing my symptoms and nerve conduction. Thousands of results would return and I spent hours each evening trying to self-diagnose, but it was a minefield of information and I couldn't pinpoint any specific diagnosis. I was going to have to wait for the outcome of the investigations, but I would still keep searching online at every available opportunity. It became an unhealthy obsession.

The physiotherapy appointment for my leg was scheduled for 23 December 2021. Great, another medical appointment two days before Christmas, which was meant to be a happy and joyful time of year. I mistakenly read that it was an in person appointment and drove to the clinic but found that it was closed. I sat myself back in the car, about to drive home when my phone started to ring. I answered and was greeted by the assessing physiotherapist who said that he wanted to discuss my symptoms and loss of strength in my right leg. I ran through all of my symptoms and he said that, as there was no pain, it was unlikely that my leg was the issue.

"So what is it then?" I asked.

Then just like that, as though I had asked him for the time, he said in a cool, calm and collected manner "Motor Neurone Disease".

"*Disease*" I shouted, "*Motor Neurone Disease?*" He responded, "Yes." I had just been told this by a medical professional (who was not qualified to diagnose) with absolutely no hesitation or compassion for what they had said. Panic and fear immediately set in as I fumbled to switch my phone to loud speaker, while at the same time frantically searching the internet for the disease and its prognosis. I don't remember much of the remaining phone call with the clinician other than shouting at him about the ease in which his words had rolled off his tongue. The results from my internet search felt like hours to arrive, but there it was in black and white "*MND is a rapidly fatal disease which kills a third of people in eighteen months. The average prognosis is between two and five years*".

I was dying. Never had I thought that would be the outcome.

I kept scrolling through and there was nothing positive. My mind raced and I couldn't compose my thoughts but I now needed to return home and tell James. As I approached the front door, I could see James through the front window in the kitchen preparing food. I came indoors and headed straight into the kitchen, nervously holding in what I was about to say. "The guy said it's Motor Neurone Disease".

James paused before he responded, "No it can't be. They've not done all the tests, so we don't know until all the tests are complete". I tried to push it to the back of my mind but it was impossible. I knew that my symptoms were the same as those listed for MND. Every waking moment was spent going into spiralling rabbit warrens of internet searches. I wished I could forget it and switch off, but I couldn't. Not even watching episodes of *Will & Grace*, my favourite TV programme could break the cycle.

Christmas was unbelievably difficult. It was a family joke that I would give the Vicar of Dibley a run for her money with my Brussels sprout addiction. Yet here I was on Christmas Day struggling to eat any of my dinner. I was full of crippling anxiety which had caused my stomach to tie itself in knots. I don't think anyone noticed, or maybe they did and they didn't want to say. All I could think was that I was sitting on a huge secret, which would result in my death. How on earth was I going to tell them and what would this do to us as a family?

As I was on washing up duty, I confided in Dad about my recent appointment. "Oh shit", he responded, clearly shocked by what I had said. We agreed that nothing else would be said until we knew for definite what it was. We visited my Aunt and Uncle along with other family members, as we often do on Christmas Day night, for the annual Boys vs Girls Trivial Pursuit game. I had driven to theirs along with James and M. After I parked up, I got out for the short walk to the front door. The temperature had clearly dropped quite significantly as my right leg muscles stiffened and locked, due to the plummeting temperature. I struggled to walk but think I hid it well. Once we were inside, my leg relaxed. While I enjoyed the games night, my mind was in overdrive and I couldn't stop thinking of the huge devastating secret I was hiding. I even thought to myself if this would be my last games night. I am never one to miss a buffet, especially at Christmas, but again I couldn't stomach eating with the crippling anxiety. Nobody joked or appeared to notice, so I think I had managed to hide it well.

New Year's Eve arrived and I tentatively made the train journey to King's College Hospital. As I arrived early, I stood outside mustering up the courage to go in. I've never liked hospitals, they are a reminder of negativity and I'd do anything to keep away from them. I had broken a bone in my leg in November 2001 as a result of landing awkwardly on a trampoline at school during a PE lesson. A trip to Bromley Hospital Accident and Emergency resulted in a six-hour wait, X-Ray and subsequent plaster cast of my entire leg. The only other time was visiting my Nan in Darent Valley Hospital when she was admitted during her cancer treatment. Sadly she continued to decline before passing away suddenly in February 2007. I chose to see her in the chapel of rest and, as much as I am pleased to have seen her sleeping, it was still a very clinical set-up, with harsh strip lighting. Hospitals are not happy places.

I slowly wandered in, found where I needed to go and checked in to the clinic. There were only a few people around, which further added to the eeriness of the situation. “Mr Hayden-Harler” a gentleman called. I followed him and prepared myself to be strapped down tightly onto a bed as I was slowly electrocuted. The truth was that the clinic was not like that at all. It had numerous screens and chairs positioned around the room. “So, what can I do for you young man?” I spent the next ten minutes going back to my initial symptoms and speaking through all of my journey so far, before ending with the bombshell that had been dropped on me a week earlier. For a man that lacked much outward emotion, he looked angry and appalled in my revelation. “I hope you’re going to complain about him?”

I said nothing. The man briefly explained what he was going to do before placing the needle in both my left and right calves. He asked me to point and flex my toes. The monitor facing me was a hive of activity with sharp lines bouncing around but, as I had no idea what this meant, I was none the wiser if this was considered normal. He then placed the needle in my arm and chin before concluding the appointment. I have always been good at reading body language and emotion, but this guy was clearly well versed in giving nothing away. I didn’t have the courage to ask what his thoughts were, so I thanked him for his time and made my way home.

January 2022 slowly arrived and I received mail inviting me to meet with an NHS Neurologist in June. Six months away. There was absolutely no way I was waiting six long months to find out what on earth was going on. I needed to find another way.

# Chapter 3: The Beginning of the End

I returned to work following the festive break absolutely wracked with anxiety, not knowing what to do. I got on well with my immediate line manager, Jane. When we were catching up, I confided in her as to the reason for all the appointments I had needed to attend. Jane reminded me of the private healthcare scheme available through my employer, and said that I should be able to receive an outcome much quicker than the agonising six month wait. That night I dug out the paperwork and made time in my diary to call them the following day.

I dialled the number with hesitation, knowing there was no going back from this. "Hello, I've been undergoing tests for the last 12 months and I've been given an appointment in six months to see a neurologist. I can't wait that long." The person I spoke to almost didn't sound surprised but assured me that, despite the neurologist currently being on leave, an appointment should be possible much sooner. I was booked in a few weeks later to see Dr Norwood at a private healthcare setting a few miles away.

I managed to put things to the back of my mind but, as each day passed, my anxiety returned and grew. The weekend finally came and I drove to the hospital, taking time to compose myself before heading in. Once I was checked in, I nervously waited to be called in for my appointment. Dr Norwood greeted me warmly and ushered me in.

I spent time going through everything right from the beginning and spoke about the last 12 months of tests which had ultimately led me there. She didn't say much but listened intently, asking questions while making extensive notes on her notepad. I listened and clung on to her every word, "There are more than 500 neurological conditions and it is my job to establish the cause. It will be a process of elimination," she said. All was not lost; perhaps there was hope that it could be another illness with similar symptoms to what I was experiencing. There was a gentle warmth to Dr Norwood and I felt confident in her approach. I suppose it takes a certain type of person to be responsible for diagnosing some pretty awful illnesses.

She joked with me that many would think my NHS test results could be located with a click of a few buttons, but sadly that isn't the case. She explained that, as time had passed since many of the tests, she wanted me to have the tests again, whilst she hunted down the original results. A follow-up appointment was made for a few weeks' time and further extensive blood tests and an MRI were requested. Before I left, she examined my body, tested my reflexes and nervous system. She relaxed each leg and foot before sharply flexing up each foot in a quick upward motion and holding the foot in place. This resulted in each of my feet shaking uncontrollably. The shaking soon stopped but my curiosity got the better of me. "What's that?" I asked. "Clonus – this is your nervous system reacting to the movement." I later Googled this and learned it is also an indication of MND.

Within a week, I was back at the hospital having my blood test. I have always had difficulty with blood tests as my veins are not prominent and they tend to hide or collapse. As expected, my veins were in incognito mode and it took two nurses to get what they needed. Next up was my MRI scan. This was pretty much the same as the first scan so I knew what to expect. I allowed my mind to calm and this helped me to relax for the duration of the scan. I returned to meet with Dr Norwood the following week; she said some results had come back but that she needed to review all the results. We scheduled the next appointment and, as I left, Dr Norwood said, "Bring James with you next time". I knew then that this was an indication that bad news was coming my way.

My immediate family were aware of the investigation works, but I tried to distance myself. I did inform them of my next appointment, explaining I would update them afterwards. Saturday 5th March soon arrived and I decided to go to my appointment alone. Whatever the outcome, I would face it by myself. Dr Norwood's desk had an extensive array of paperwork which I presumed were my results. She began to explain that my blood test had shown I was low in folic acid, so recommended that I start taking 5mg each day. Other than that nothing significant or concerning was evident but there was a sign that a protein was in my blood which indicated some of my muscles were working harder than normal. Stupidly I thought that was the worst of it. I clung onto her every word as I waited with bated breath. The MRI had been inconclusive and showed nothing of concern.

Dr Norwood paused for a few moments and made direct eye contact, "Following a review of your results and repeated examinations, I am sorry to inform you that I believe your symptoms are as a result of Motor Neurone Disease". That was it, life was over.

I don't remember much more of what was said, as a montage of my life flashed before my eyes. I started to think of all the people I needed to tell and the pain this would cause them. I clearly hadn't been listening to the neurologist as it suddenly began to hit me as tears streamed down my face. She asked if I had understood what had been said, as I abruptly blurted out "Well that's me dead then".

She tried to comfort me, "Sam, some people bumble through life for years not achieving much. You will now go on to live your life and do lots in the next few years and accomplish so much more". I have held those words close to me, knowing I have done exactly that. Dr Norwood's words were imprinted in my mind forever more. She asked how long I wanted off work but I didn't want any time off. All I would do is sit and cry, feeling sorry for myself. Nope, that wasn't an option for me. I wanted normality and routine. She double checked with me, as though I hadn't heard a word that had been spoken. I affirmed my understanding but perhaps I seemed too accepting of the diagnosis. A prescription was written for Mirtazapine to help with sleep and anxiety, in addition to folic acid. Dr Norwood also recommended taking Riluzole, the only drug in the UK licensed for MND patients. It would not cure the illness but would possibly help slow down the progression of the disease. She provided assurance that she had diagnosed others of a similar age who had been prescribed Riluzole and who had lived a long time with it.

She wanted to see me for a final time in a few weeks before handing me over to an NHS neurologist. I now needed to begin the painful task of telling my loved ones. I left the car park quickly and knew I needed to call Dad to tell him. He answered after a few rings and asked how I had got on. "Dad, it's the worst news possible. It's MND". "Oh no" he responded, clearly dumbfounded from my declaration. I could hear the shock in his voice. Dad offered to come and see me but I knew that I needed to be away from the house.

I returned home and found James in the kitchen. "It's Motor Neurone Disease," I sobbed as James cuddled me, attempting to console me. I know he went into poker face mode, trying not to show emotion following my outburst. I had only told two people of my news now, but both times it had felt like a dagger though my heart. I knew that I couldn't cope with telling others because it became more painful each time. I don't know how but I managed to compose myself as we left the house to drive to see my family. I stayed silent for the 30-mile drive as internally I was numb, but my mind was racing, thinking of all the people I needed to tell, how I was going to say it and just how and when the disease would progress. I felt scared in not being able to control it.

I sat in an armchair not knowing what to say to everyone. I don't remember much of what was said, I had only been told that my illness was terminal a few hours before. I cried a lot, saying how guilty I felt in that I had caused this. Mum, Dad, my sister Becky and James tried to reassure me that I should carry no guilt, and that I had absolutely no control over the illness. I was emotionally numb. We stayed for a little while before heading home to try and work through the first few days of my new life. I went to bed earlier than James, searching the internet on my phone to try to comfort myself and find younger people who had been diagnosed, but I couldn't see anyone like me. This made me feel even more isolated, I just wanted to know that I was going to be okay.

Thanks to the effects of Mirtazapine, which had a mild sedative effect, I became sleepy. As I lay in bed I could hear James downstairs uncontrollably wailing. This hurt. I couldn't console him because of my own emotional turmoil. What on earth could I do? I could no longer think of the future; there was no future for me.

The following day, I knew that I needed to start telling those closest to me, but doing so face to face was just too painful right now. I spent hours drafting a WhatsApp message, because how exactly do you tell people that you're dying? I must've rewritten the message many times before I eventually hit "send". I watched as replies were received over the following days. Many did not know what to say, but assured me that I was not alone, offering anything they could to help us as we navigated uncharted territory. The love and support kept my spirits high and kept me going.

It was my choice to return to work on the Monday. It was less than 48 hours since my diagnosis, but I needed normality and routine. I could have taken several months off work but I know it would have been easy to let the disease get the better of me. I didn't want that. My body was out of control and had other plans for me, so I needed to keep hold of things that were still in my control. Work had always been a constant for me and I loved my job, which is why I chose to keep working. I honestly believe my longevity with the illness is because I have carried on working full-time. MND brings with it many unknowns; in the early days, I genuinely believed I would stop working at the end of 2022, but thankfully that has not been the case.

I called Jane and just about kept the tears at bay as I told her of my devastating news, eventually bursting in to tears. "Oh flower," she said. I had got on well with Jane since we first met in 2017 when she interviewed me. It hadn't taken long for me to see that she was a people person through and through. Over the years, I had many a lengthy chat with her about life and knew she always had my back. She was and still is one of life's good people – a good egg. I spoke with her and said that I wanted to carry on and to move forward as if nothing had happened. My job involved me visiting and speaking with people in their homes, so we agreed to touch base often to risk assess my situation. I made it clear that I was happy for her to notify the team, but that I wanted no special treatment or to be treated any differently. I was and still am the same person and certainly wanted to carry on with my chin held high.

While professionally, I had made my preferences clear, I needed to somehow tell others in my personal life of my news but I didn't know how. I knew that it would be easier and less painful to not have to keep repeating myself but didn't know how this was possible. One evening James said, "Why don't you use the YouTube channel to share it?" I had totally forgotten our YouTube vlog "Daddy, Dad & Me" in which I had openly documented and shared our journey to adoption and through parenthood. It meant that I needed to record a painfully emotive moment, but also that I wouldn't have to keep repeating myself.

# CHAPTER 4: WHY ME?

*HI EVERYBODY. I'M NOT my usual happy self because something's recently happened and it's shattered my world. As you know we've obviously got a blog and vlog and it's one of the ways that I find I can connect with people. It's just that this story is not a story, and that every time I repeat it, it gets harder and harder to say, because it makes it a reality.*

*I wanted to create this video as maybe as a way of documenting things as they go and just to let other people know. To take you back to last year, I started noticing that parts of my body were weaker and didn't feel normal. I felt like I had less strength. It's been a long time coming, but something happened around Christmas which kind of sparked something and I've kind of not been the same. I've been undergoing various investigations and tests and sadly I have to let people know that I've recently been diagnosed with Motor Neurone Disease.*

*It's a progressive disease and I've noticed the changes in me but it's initially it's one of those that's very hidden. You wouldn't look at me and think anything was going on. I've recently had it diagnosed and all I can say is that I start living from now. I've already said to my team, the health people behind it, I don't want to know the kind of prognosis. I have to start living my life. I'm already putting together my bucket list and I know how I feel. Telling my family and friends has been the most awful thing in the entire world. I just want it known, because it is so rare; even the neurologist said for someone my age it is rare; there are people out there but not many younger than me.*

*It's usually onset later in life and I'm going to do my absolute hardest to raise money for MND, because it's so underfunded and the research around it and things that can help and treatments. It's not curable but there are things in place they can do to slow it down. I apologise if this triggers anybody or upsets people, but it's kind of the easiest way that I know in which to tell others and it's out there. I don't have to worry about that anymore, not that I would worry anyway.*

*I just want people to know that that's the reality sometimes of some people's life and that if you see my friends and family starting to crack, there is a reason why. Emotionally, I'm all over the place at the moment. I know that better days will come, but I have to kind of take things as they are. It's not great news but I wanted to tell people so that it has been said. I don't have to keep on explaining myself if someone asks if I'm okay. Every day is different, like yesterday I was absolutely fine and then bang, another day it could be the reality of it, or you hear a song, or something...*

*I just want to carry on being as normal as possible while I can and adapt into my new normal. When you're faced with a terminal illness... I've reevaluated a lot of things I honestly worried or thought about, and seen they are now so insignificant. It's taught me a lot already and I really am living in the moment. I look at things so differently and I would just say be kind to each other because honestly you never know when this moment or something can just absolutely change. Stop worrying about getting the perfect Instagram selfie or photo and look at those around you. One day those things can change.*

*I don't want sympathy, it's about support and understanding at this moment and, for those who do know my friends and family, please be kind to them. Let's start living."*

Done. I uploaded the video and, in a few minutes, it was live. I then shared it on my social media so it could be seen by family and friends. It wasn't long at all until I started receiving messages of love and support and hundreds of comments. This really helped to get me through the days and weeks of my new unwanted life. As much as I craved normality, I now realise how emotionally numb I was. I could no longer look to or plan for the future; instead, all I could do was to focus on the present. I would still have moments when I would zone out and let my mind wander dangerously into the future, thinking about what life would be like when I was paralysed. I still have these thoughts; however, what I have come to understand is that things may not be as bad as I first imagined. I remain hopeful.

When you are hit with a terminal diagnosis, I've learnt that it's entirely normal to become fixated on death. For pretty much all of the six months post-diagnosis I believed I'd be dead within a year. After all, that's what the statistics allude to, so it must be true. I needed to regain control of my life and something that would allow me to do exactly that was planning and preparing for my own funeral. In just the same way you would plan a birthday party, I made plans for my final moments. It has given me great comfort to know my final wishes have been documented. Sadly, I have experienced deaths since I was young, and most of them hadn't known they were going to die. I didn't want my loved ones to have to guess what my wishes would be at an already difficult time following a loss. So I set the wheels in motion and started to document everything on my MacBook. From the clothes I want to wear, the cologne I want to be spritzed with, to writing my own eulogy and carefully selecting music, I've prepared it all. I also arranged my own funeral plan which is now all paid for, giving me further comfort that this will not be a financial burden for anyone. We need to normalise something that is inevitable for us all.

Once the initial shock settled after a few weeks, I started to notice a shift in my energy. Yes, I was angry, upset and confused. I could choose to withdraw from the world, but that didn't feel right for me. I needed to turn this god-awful situation into something positive and meaningful, I just needed to figure out how to make that happen. It soon came to me that I needed to be the person I had been unable to find while I was undergoing investigations for my symptoms. What meant more to me was my legacy, how I would be remembered. I wanted to know that, despite everything, I did everything I possibly could. That was the vow I made to myself.

I knew that, for others to see me, I needed to be willing to publicly share parts of my life that would allow the world to catch a glimpse of life, navigating a degenerative terminal illness. This resulted in "Sam & The Bucket List" being created online; a space that would allow me to share the highs and lows of living with MND, plus showing that I could still be happy.

One evening James asked, "So what is it that you want to do? What's on your bucket list?" Of course I had had the pleasure of experiencing big life moments, but I had never really thought about what I wanted to achieve before "kicking the bucket". Over the course of the next few weeks I listed the moments I had already completed and went on to note what I wanted to tick off. To add a humorous touch I called my bucket list blog "When Life Hands You Lemons". Number one on my list is of course, "Make fresh lemonade"! I shared this online and was overwhelmed by people approaching me, who wanted to help in any way they could. The list gave me purpose and a sense of accomplishment. It also helped to maintain my focus.

By now a month or so had passed and it was time to see Dr. Norwood for the final time. She had previously explained that, while she would want to be part of my NHS team, this would not be possible due to the jurisdiction that she covers. This time, I took James with me and it was pretty clear that Dr Norwood was quite taken aback with my having such a positive outlook so soon. I spoke with her about what I had been up to and the creation of my bucket list, along with my intention to publicly share my story.

She briefly mentioned the work of the Motor Neurone Disease Association (MNDA), and said that I might find their Thumbprint magazine useful and want to speak with someone there. In the moment, I couldn't think about that; it would have felt like information overload and that's the last thing I wanted. We spoke about the prescribed medication and how this was helping with anxiety and with getting some decent sleep. Finally she said that I would now be referred to the NHS, where a multi-disciplinary team would be put together to care for me, reassuring me that it would all happen very quickly. We left the hospital and it was now over to us to make the most of life from this moment on.

Around this time I was contacted by Nikki, the mum of one of our son's school friends. She suggested organising a fundraiser gala with all proceeds going to the MNDA. I thought about it briefly and my answer was an excited "Yes." A local venue, The Alexandra Suite, generously gifted us the venue for the night, and we then needed to arrange entertainment and the all-important raffle and auction prizes. We spent most evenings over the next five months ensuring an action-packed schedule and spent many hours relentlessly reaching out to both local and national businesses, asking if they would sponsor the gala or gift us prizes. The organisation of the gala allowed me to focus my time and energy in the early months but it also gave me the opportunity to share my story.

I had several news articles written about my diagnosis and my positive outlook on life. It wasn't long before I was being contacted by others in a similar position; I was so thankful that I could help others by sharing my experience.

# Chapter 5: New Beginnings

True to her word, I received mail inviting me to meet with my new neurologist, Dr Ellis, at Darent Valley Hospital. This time, I wasn't filled with dread or panic. I was already in receipt of my membership of the MND club. While I was never a fan of visiting hospitals, I had a sense of calm about me and was curious about the meeting.

My appointment date soon came around. At this time, my symptoms were still not especially visible. I still had the use of my arms and legs, and was able to walk unaided. Before meeting Dr Ellis, I had my observations taken which included weight and blood pressure. As this was my first visit, I had to repeat my symptom history before an examination. It was a pretty swift meeting, but I preferred it that way. I was told that Riluzole, the medication that may slow its progression, could be quite harsh on the liver, and I would thus be required to have frequent blood tests. Oh deep joy.

Dr Ellis is friendly, warm and gentle in nature, I can imagine being a neurologist involves diagnosing some pretty horrific illnesses. It is tough job I am sure. She comforted me when she said, "The stats you see are based upon those diagnosed in their 50s and above. They are not based on someone of your age". This is something that has stuck with me. It gives me hope that my progression will allow me to be here for as long as possible, and that's all I could ever wish for.

It was also explained to me that my new team, consisting of a specialist MND nurse and Occupational Therapist, would visit me at home and give feedback to Dr Ellis ensuring a joined-up approach. I felt and still do feel cared for. I have gone on to learn that not everybody in the UK has had the same experience. There have been people who have had to fight for any level of care at all. It shouldn't be a postcode lottery; all MND warriors should get the same care regardless of location.

Dr Ellis said I would be referred to a respiratory unit in London. What? As I was aware, my breathing was fine as far but now I would be under the spotlight for this, and so soon. The fear must've shown in my eyes and so it was explained that they would want to know what my baseline observations, such as how strong my diaphragm was, oxygen and carbon dioxide levels and lung function. There is something about the respiratory system and MND that made me realise this was going to be relentless and unforgiving.

While meeting Dr Ellis went smoothly, it felt like a reminder of being told I had MND all over again. I have since gone on to get the appointments out the way as soon as possible, so I can move on with life. After each visit, I receive a letter outlining my symptoms, progression and what was discussed. I never read them, I know what was said and they get filed straight away. They serve as a constant reminder that I do not need. I know what I have, I am the occupier of this body. At the end of the meeting, Dr Ellis said the appointments would be scheduled every three months, but these could change should I need to see her sooner. I went on my way and back to daily life, where I would be waiting to hear from my care team.

Up until this point, I had not wanted to engage with the MND Association. As I said, I was worried it would be information overload. I was scared by their website, because all I saw was statistics and words like death and fatal. That was too much to see. I soon received an email from Esther who had seen some of my posts online. A few email exchanges between us led to a long telephone call in which I shared my story with her. I made it clear that I didn't want to have statistics in front of me and they have stuck to that since day one. Then I said that I was happy to share my story publicly, I also spoke with Emily at the Association. She had helped others in sharing their stories and becoming involved with projects and campaigns. She went on to explain that the Association was often contacted by external parties as well as internal departments and asked if I would be happy to be involved when these opportunities arose. This was my opportunity to make a difference, and for those diagnosed in younger generations to be seen and heard. "Absolutely", I said. This was the start of my journey with the Association, which has led to being involved with many projects and campaigns.

Around July 2022 I was visited by Kim and Katrina, my assigned Occupational Therapist and Specialist MND nurse. They were both lovely and put me at ease, as my symptoms were not significant. There was nothing I really needed from them at this stage. I did however want to forward plan, as not everything was readily available and some services involved jumping through many hoops. As my right foot had started to weaken (known as foot drop) and was a little more obvious,

I asked if there was anything that could be done. Kim said that she'd refer me to an NHS service that would be able to provide a foot brace. I got the brace several months later but never used it again as it was too difficult to fit myself. I also mentioned to Katrina that I had heard of a Personal Independence Payment (PIP), but wasn't sure if I was eligible. She agreed to would investigate, which she did and, within a month, I was being paid the enhanced rate. I'd definitely recommend speaking with your specialist to see what is available, because nobody tells you unless you find out for yourself! My general observations were taken and they both went on their way, agreeing to return in several months.

I soon received my appointment for the Lane Fox Respiratory Unit at St Thomas's Hospital, London, for 19th August 2022. Great! Two days after my $36^{th}$ birthday and the day before the Gala. I really didn't know what to expect for my first visit and despite searching online I couldn't find any information that may have alleviated those fears. So I went along with an open and curious mind.

Thanks to the busy summer in London and a well-timed tube strike, I was typically late for my appointment, which made me all the more anxious. Nevertheless I arrived, and it wasn't long before my height and weight were recorded, before I was taken in to see the consultant. They hooked me up to a monitor which measured my oxygen and carbon dioxide levels, along with my heart rate. I looked at the numbers and had no clue what they meant. Then they wanted to measure lung capacity and the strength of my diaphragm. A plastic bullet was inserted into my nostril while the other was covered. I was told to take a sharp and sudden intake of air through my nostril. "You have a large snip," I was informed. Ooo-err Missus! What this actually meant was that, at this point, my respiratory system was strong. My anxiety diminished as they said they wouldn't need to see me for six months. Phew. I could now turn my attention to the Gala which was fast approaching. On the way home I bought M a pen depicting a soldier wearing the famous black hat. He still uses it occasionally and it always reminds me of that day.

The Gala day was finally here and it was time to put everything together. A few last-minute changes had to be sorted throughout the day, as all hands were on deck to dress and prepare the venue, ready for our guests to arrive from six o'clock. All the hard work over the last five months had led to this day. We had an army of helpers to get everything sorted and a few last-minute changes. We had sold more than 70 tickets for our three course dinner in addition to local and national organisations sponsoring the guest tables.

Our guests enjoyed a glass of fizz before being pictured on the red carpet. While waiting for the remainder of the guests to arrive, they had the opportunity to buy raffle tickets and bid in a silent auction. We had been lucky to have been gifted a huge amount of prizes including a signed drum skin from Coldplay, a private holiday rental and event tickets. Later on in the evening, guests were taken by surprise when some of the guests and waiters revealed themselves to be professional singers! The delight and shock on guests' faces was priceless. It had everyone on their feet and certainly made it a night to remember, which is exactly what I had wanted it to be. Comedienne Jo Enright entertained our guests ahead of our live auction, before we wrapped up the night with live music. We were shattered come the end of the night, but it was a huge success with lots of funds being donated. After some number-crunching at the end of the night, we were extremely proud to say that £12,009.54 had been raised and donated to the MND Association. A resounding success that would go on to help so many and do so much.

I enjoyed some downtime after the Gala, as it had taken a lot of time and effort to make it happen. Around this time I saw Kim and Katrina again. The weakness had continued progressing and I was encouraged to apply for a blue badge for disabled parking. They also made a referral for a manual wheelchair. I was told the wheelchair should be quick as I was marked as "urgent"; however it took a long six months. Thankfully I did not need it urgently but this taught me that some services had exceptionally long wait times. I had the same experience with the blue badge application, which also took six months to be granted. Again my specialist provided them with a letter noting my symptoms, which ultimately sped up the application.

There was a lot happening around this time as we knew that it was getting harder for me to wash and dress myself. At home, it was also harder to navigate stairs, with a heightened risk of falling. The decision was made to sell up and find a suitable property, along with my parents and sister. The difficulty was finding suitable properties for six people and our Dachshund, Ralph. Many were discounted by us all either because of location or because the space simply wouldn't work. To find a property that could accommodate six, along with being accessible, was not going to be easy.

Eventually we sold our cottage and my parents sold their property, although the sale had fallen through for both of us at one point. We found a house and, while it wasn't perfect, it had ticked more boxes than the others we'd seen. It had lots of potential which is what made it the ideal choice. Despite there being multiple challenges along the way, the sales eventually went through and the move was all set for April 2022.

We had to consider the fact that adopted children have already suffered significant loss in their life as a result of moving, and this is traumatic for them. We knew that we would have to navigate the move sensitively as M would be changing schools; he had moved many times in his life, and there had been significant losses each and every time. We had kept in close contact with his school and, nearer to the time of the move, they spent a lot of time preparing him for the transition to his new school. We knew he was sad to be leaving, but we had explained why we needed to move.

The day of the move came and, as the removals firm had already removed items the day before, they didn't need to do as much on the day. I was still driving then, so was taking M to his new school; we had finally taken the decision to change schools at the Easter break. He said goodbye to his room and the rest of the house. He was heartbroken and emotional but he needed to be able to do this and for us to not hide away from it. The move went well but it took weeks to find a new home for most things. Now I could live downstairs, as our bedroom is on the ground floor. We also had an en suite wet room which would make showering much easier and safer.

By now, my arms were continuing to deteriorate. Although I'm fiercely independent and had found inventive ways to shower and dress myself, I knew that before long I was going to need help, even though for now I was okay. As we had moved quite a distance it meant that some of my team had to change. It took time for the adjustments to be made, but after a few months my new team were all set. I keep in regular communication with my team as and when I needed their assistance.

As we needed to modernise and adapt the wet room for my needs, we involved the council. Despite reassuring me that my case was urgent, it took multiple escalations to senior management for any kind of progress to be made. At its worst, I was sending daily emails picking out the continual failures. I really had to fight my corner, which angered me because it was clear there were many others like me, stuck in a weave of red tape. It still took a year to complete... but it is matched to my needs. The wash and dry toilet means I retain some dignity and independence.

To continue with my mission of raising funds and awareness, my lovely friend Graeme got to work along with his many talented friends to hold my very own music festival, "SamFest". In the run up to the event, I took part in several live radio interviews. It took place on 15 April 2023 at The Egg Theatre, Bath and was an action-packed day with an eclectic mix of live music and performance. Thanks to the generosity of others, the festival raised more than £2,800 for the MND Association.

I chose to publicly share my own experience of living with MND to raise awareness and to educate others, especially those from the younger generations and LGBTQIA+ community. I have been involved with the MND Associations "MND Matters" podcast for

Pride month, in addition to James and I speaking at the association's internal Pride event about our own experiences.

I was extremely honoured to have been chosen by the MNDA to take part in and be photographed by Richard Cannon for an online exhibition to raise awareness of those living with MND. The exhibition captured people at different phases to show how, at first it can be hidden, how the disease affects the body in the advanced stages, and the level of care needed to support people.

I featured in the '"TakeOverMND'"January 2023 fundraising campaign, as well as the association's annual CEO appeal, which raised a staggering £239,999.

The MND Association arranged for me to engage with the cast of *Coronation Street,* playing a pivotal role in developing their storyline featuring MND, which ran from April 2023 for a year and a half. As a young gay man diagnosed, I shared my own experiences with them to help shape the portrayal of Paul, played by Peter Ash, a character whose story ran almost parallel to my reality. It was also helpful to understand how Paul's husband, played by Daniel Brocklebank, navigated their journey and the tough reality faced as Paul's carer and the strain this placed upon their relationship.

I met with Peter and Daniel, visiting "the Street" and shared my experience for the MND community by writing in their quarterly members' magazine, Thumbprint. This also led to a national television interview on *Good Morning Britain* where Peter and I spoke about the experience. You can catch the interview on YouTube. In supporting many campaigns and projects, I was chosen as the UK representative for the International Alliance of ALS/MND's "March of Faces", a celebration of individuals living with MND who have made a valuable and significant contribution to the MND community.

In helping others who are navigating their journey to non-invasive ventilation, I took part in filming a patient story for Home Mechanical Ventilation and their #AddingLifeToYears campaign. The annual Marie Curie Great Daffodil Appeal saw me supporting their social media and being a voice for those living with life-limiting illnesses. Elements of my story have been featured in a number of the Association's publications, including their Sex and Relationships information booklet.

Despite the symptomatic development of MND, I try to leave a positive impact for the MND community by sharing my experiences, giving a voice to challenges that many do not talk about, such as how to deal with eating when you cannot use your hands, and the difficulties of getting dressed.

I have also been able to share my story with articles written in The Sun, The Mirror, Metro and Daily Mail.

I am relentless in my desire to continue spreading awareness and seize every opportunity to make a difference. I continue to feature within MND Association literature, representing young men affected by MND, and have spoken at important events, including the Mid-Kent Round table event, helping to forge the way forward to change the prognosis of MND.

More recently, I participated in workshops dedicated to the Association's current brand review. I gave a voice to both the MND and LGBTQIA+ community to share my thoughts and wishes for the evolution of the brand, ensuring the diverse lived experiences of those affected by the disease were heard and considered.

My respiratory appointments come along every three months and they cause me significant anxiety, I think because of the serious effects it can have on the body. My results did change and I was recommended to start overnight ventilation. It's important to mention that the non-invasive ventilator does not provide me with oxygen, but a blast of air to support the weakened muscles. The reality is that the results will never improve and will only decrease. I do feel the benefit of ventilation, but is it still the appointment I hate seeing in my diary. I am at the point now where I am introducing some ventilation during the day. The illness constantly reminds me to live a day at a time.

I firmly believe my longevity with the disease comes from working, which gives me purpose every day.

# Chapter 6: Looking Back

17th August 1986 saw me enter the world a little earlier than my parents, Jayne and Graham, had planned. Due to Mum's diabetes I was born a month early at Queen Mary's Hospital, Sidcup. I spent time in an incubator before eventually being allowed to go home. Weirdly enough this same hospital would be where 34 years later I would need to undergo testing following weakness in my hand.

We lived in a small bungalow in a relatively small town, St Paul's Cray, not far from Orpington, Kent. Along with my parents and my sister Becky, who had been born several years earlier, home was a happy place. We were given the freedom to be who we wanted to be. Those were the days when you could happily leave the doors open. It was normal for Becky and me to be out playing from dawn until dusk. Our weekly pocket money would see us making a frantic dash to visit Raj's newsagent nearby and to get as many penny sweets as we could, back when sweets were actually a penny! We would then either head to the park opposite or take a slow walk home, stuffing our faces with as many sweets as we could. We loved being outdoors and, as our garden was over 100 feet long, there was a huge amount of space for us to play in. I could often be found climbing my way up the huge apple tree and making my own den. We didn't have hundreds of toys like the kids nowadays, but we made do with what we had. This was long before mobile phones or the internet so we made our own fun and rarely got bored.

Mum and Dad were both Civil Servants, working for the Inland Revenue, now known as HMRC. As they both worked hard, they would drop us off with our childminder Sheila who cared for us and would walk us to school. We loved our time with Sheila, especially during the school holidays. She also worked part-time to assist the elderly with their food shopping and we loved visiting them and helping. There was one lady who was my favourite, as on each and every visit she would insist on us picking out a few pear drops from her sweet jar. Heaven!

I have loved Christmas for as long as I can remember, and proudly won a fancy dress competition dressed as a present during my time at primary school. Waiting to open presents at a young age was absolute torture; now as a parent myself, it's great to watch. When we were around five, the waiting got too much so I crept into Becky's room in the early hours and we devised a plan. Fast forward a few hours to being caught red-handed by Mum and Dad once we had opened all of our presents. They were far from impressed. I also perfected the wetting of the present corner to see if I could catch a glimpse of what was inside! Three decades on and while I can't open presents, I still cherish family time at this time of year. One of the most special memories was having the entire family huddled around playing my new Scalextric. Christmas at this time would also see us going into Mum and Dad's workplace once school had ended for the holidays. We would often visit and got to know people there. They threw great office parties and it was another chance to run around the office. It all made for a really happy childhood.

Family has always been important to me and I consider we were lucky to have our grandparents around while we grew from children into adults, and to have spent lots of time with them. My paternal grandparents, Ron and Violet, lived in a beautiful house in Petts Wood, which had a stunning landscaped garden and a large hand-built pond full of Koi. We would visit every Friday after school and Grandad would tell his tales of war. Nan was a kind, generous soul with a cracking sense of humour and I loved watching her winding up Grandad. She didn't always say a lot but she used her razor-sharp wit and precision timing to bring lots of laughter to her world. She adored having grandchildren, and we would look forward to receiving her weekly sweet treat offering of fruit pastilles; we all loved her company. I will always be thankful to her for teaching me my times tables. Sadly Nan was diagnosed with dementia; it was really difficult to watch her fade away from being the person I knew. She passed in 2010, which hit me hard. However, since then I have seen the positive effects she had on me
.

My maternal grandparents, Vera and Cyril, lived in Dartford with my aunt. We would visit every few weekends and spend several hours there, often playing in the garden or on the communal green at the front. Nan would buy us felt art sets from the local market, and we would to get cracking with these while the adults chatted away. We would occasionally spend the weekend with them; we loved the electric blanket being left on in winter and multiple thick blankets. I could barely move, but I was toasty! Come the morning, three adults, two children and a dining table were slotted into their small kitchen like a game of Tetris. A full on fry up for breakfast ensued, which set us up for the day ahead. Nan taught us how to knit, among many other things, and I would watch in awe at the speed at which she knitted, while watching television or engaging in conversation. She wouldn't miss a stitch! She loved to cook and was known in the family for making potent pickled onions that had some serious flavour and a strong bite! Nan was a strong, assertive woman who put down firm boundaries; she was not a person that I wanted to cross. We respected those boundaries, but of course tried to push them, as children do.

Raglan Primary School was a very happy place and time for me. It was a time of happy memories and the best years of my life. I respected my teachers and their individual ways. Some were creative, others more academic. My reception teacher, Mrs Scholes, was a gentle, quiet older lady and, on my very first day of reception, I was the first in the classroom, so she read to me. I think that this moment allowed me to love reading books from an early age. Young minds absorb information like a sponge; not only was I receiving an education, but I took a lot from my primary years from my teachers. Most of them were gentle and caring, much like Miss Honey in Matilda. Mrs Meakin was a caring teacher, but she also instilled the fear of God in you with her booming voice, which would make your hair stand on end if you so much as dared be rude to her. She wasn't scary, but the boundaries were very clear and I didn't disobey her.

I tell a lie... one afternoon, a performance was taking place in the assembly hall on the stage, which backed onto a storage room. Several of us had left our classroom to fetch something from the storage area and could hear and see that the stage was mid-performance. Our inquisitive minds clearly got the better of us and so we climbed on chairs and peered over the top of the rear stage wall, not realising our heads were now in full view of the audience. I locked eyes with Mrs Meakin and, despite trying to run away and escape in double time, she caught us. We were suitably told off and I never crossed her again. I think.

I wasn't a popular kid but I made friends easily and was happy to gravitate to others. In my junior years, I joined the schools eco-warrior club, run by Mrs Pritchard. She was a teacher who was easily in her late 60s and who had a passion for making the planet a happier and cleaner place. I would go to the club once a week and there were different tasks to complete, from litter picking to spreading the word. I'm happy to have been part of this in the early 1990s and to have been part of a generation that wanted to care for the planet. Before leaving in 1997 the school got awards for its forward-thinking environmental actions, something I like to think I was part of. It also had its own quiet garden for us to enjoy, years before the world became more attuned to mental health.

Outside school, I joined the Cubs briefly before moving up to the Scouts. I became part of the Fifth Bromley Group and spent a few years really getting to grips with Scouting life. It gave me a good grounding for discipline and being respectful of others, as well as learning all about setting up camp and doing things for the community. I loved going on a number of camps, which made me more independent, while learning general life skills certainly made me streetwise. I remember one camp, sitting around the campfire and looking up to the crystal clear night sky as a comet shot across it. Just beautiful.

It was around nine years old that I developed an interest in gymnastics, as some coaches of a local club visited my school. I signed up and every Friday night I was taken to Ravensborne Secondary school. Over the next three years I worked hard and ended up competing regionally, winning bronze and silver in consecutive years. This was a great discipline to learn, and I was able to competently navigate the beam, floor work and the horse. I wish I carried on with it, as I believe I could have gone far. Instead I ended up leaving in 1998 because my interests had changed since starting secondary school and I lost interest for it. Who knows where I would have ended up, but I'm glad to still have my medals some 30 years later.

1996 was the start of my final year at Raglan, as I headed into year six. Being in the top year in school made me feel invincible. Despite the unknown ahead of me in terms of my secondary education, this final year carried with it extra responsibilities. (I was a lunchtime monitor for the library – I got all the glam jobs). We were trusted by teachers and pupils, but also had activities and things planned, as we prepared to leave primary education.

My Nan Violet spent time with Becky and me over the years recalling her memories of living through wartime. I always listened intently, as she handed down to us her stories of being evacuated to Uckfield, East Sussex and what it was like to live through this time. One afternoon she got out lots of photo albums, telling us about our family pictured in the visibly aged black and white photographs. There were also photographs of her and my Grandad in Ashdown Forest, a place they visited often (despite my grandad saying they never went there). Following her passing in 2010 we visited the forest and planted a flower in her memory. My interest in the Second World War was because of Nan, so when a school visit was planned for the Imperial War Museum I knew that I would enjoy it. I have loved history and still to this day enjoy museums or historical programmes, and this has been handed down to M, who is also keen to learn more history.

Towards the end of year six, we had a week's residential trip to the Isle of Wight planned. As this was the first time away from home for many of us, we were very excitable. I remember the coach of 60 loud children leaving school and the delight of the parents' faces as they waved us goodbye. It was a great week away and was packed with historical trips, sand-sculpture competitions and happy times with friends. Sadly, when I visited it again a few years ago, lots of places had closed or changed.

When we returned to school for the summer term, it was time for us to prepare for our leavers' assembly and our performance of The Jungle Book. As I had been going to dance classes at school I found myself cast as a dancing monkey. (Some may consider this rather apt.) I was going to miss Raglan, a place that had allowed me to explore my creativity, nurtured me and had been formative in learning many things about myself and others. We performed our show to the school one July afternoon. The evening performance would be to our family and, as we parked outside school that night, Nan (Violet) handed me a present. It was an autograph book for me to get autographs from my friends. She was such a generous and thoughtful person; she had written her own poem on the inside cover. I still have the book today.

All my grandparents came along with Mum, Dad and Becky. The performance went perfectly. We all said a tearful "Goodbye Raglan" as we told the audience which school we were going to. Thankfully, there were a handful of us going to my secondary school, which would hopefully ease the transition.

The last day of school soon came around and I had my autograph book along with my school shirt, ready to be signed. A rounders match was scheduled: Year Six vs The Teachers. I'm pleased to say we beat them and it was a fantastic memory to have from our last day. Finally, after school, a lot of us went to an end of school party at our friend Tom's house. It was an emotional day as the reality was that many of us would part ways and not see or speak to each other again. None of us could be fully prepared for what was to come, but we now had to fly the nest and find our feet.

# Chapter 7: The Teenage Years

A brown blazer and trousers along with a yellow shirt was not the best combination of colours for a school uniform, but it was something I would have to live with for the next five years. September 1997 saw me start at Darrick Wood. Becky had started there a few years earlier. It was comforting to know we would both be at the same school.

I was in "March" form and these would be people who would grow with me and change in many ways over the course of our secondary schooling. I was quite nervous having been plucked from the comfort of primary school and thrust into the unfamiliarity of my new school. It took months to find my feet and adjust to a full-on schedule of lessons and homework. Then, just as I started to feel stability, things felt different.

In some ways I had always known I was different, but this had always been my normal. I had always been able to express myself and my early childhood meant I was free to discover who I was. I don't recall how young I was when I started to realise that I was attracted to the same sex, but I think it may have been around eleven or so that I felt different. I certainly didn't know this would start a huge journey towards understanding my sexuality. Around this time I decided to leave the Scouts and instead joined the Sea Cadets, as mum's friend was an Officer and thought I would enjoy it. I quickly became friends with others and it became somewhere that was a safe place every Monday and Thursday. I took part in 'Flag Week', a fundraiser that saw cadets out in the local community every night, collecting money, which would support the cadets in various ways. The week would end with cadets being positioned in a very busy Bromley High Street collecting donations from passers-by. I was dressed in our smart naval wear, which was immediately recognisable. I saw others from my new school and this is where my bullying started.

I have never been one to follow the crowd. I like doing my own thing and preferred the company of females, which is why at school I gravitated to them. This coupled with my sea cadet involvement resulted in name calling me "sailor boy". How original. I initially ignored the name calling but it soon turned to derogatory names such as "gay boy", "faggot" or "poof". Despite my best efforts to shrug these comments off and ignore them, they started to get to me, before things worsened. At the same time as trying to receive an education, I was now having to battle with my bullies and try to avoid them the best I could. Some days it was easier than others but there were very few classes in which I felt as though I could outwardly be myself. I found it interesting that, without their friends, they were pretty powerless... but as soon as they were in a group the onslaught of abuse began. I did my best to try and avoid them, but that wasn't always easy.

It took time to make any meaningful friendships. However, when I went to my English lesson one day, there was a new teacher who introduced a new seating plan. By the time I reached the classroom door, I was told that I would be sitting next to Jo. I had never spoken to her before, but had seen her around school. She was self-confident and assertive and I really wasn't sure how sitting next to her would go. I was fully expecting to be ignored or picked on. Thankfully neither happened. Initially we exchanged very little conversation but after a short while we realised that we had more in common than we had initially realised. We started to spend more time together outside of English lessons. Come year eight and nine, I cherished our friendship as we would spend more time together. We would have other lessons together and soon became inseparable as we began to hang out after sc hool too.

Performing Arts was a safe place, not only could I be self-expressive there, but my teacher, Mrs Heath, was openly gay and was not shy in coming forward. She would not tolerate anyone who was unkind. Jo and I spent time around the drama department and, despite being in lower years, Mrs Heath let us join trips for the sixth form to London to see shows. This is where my love of theatre began. All of my other lessons had at least one person in them who would taunt or bully me. The bullying worsened over time and it started to get physical. I was hit, kicked, and tripped up, as well as having objects thrown at me. A blackboard rubber was once thrown at the back of my head, which resulted in significant bruising – my Dad saw it later that day, resulting in him writing a letter of complaint to the school. My form teacher was far from impressed and spoke to those involved, essentially threatening them, saying that if it didn't stop, he would stop it. I knew then that he had my back. Thankfully no further physical violence came my way, but the name calling was present every single day until I left in 2002.

I didn't enjoy my time at secondary school as there were very few positive experiences – most of the time I was being picked on. I did however have a great time when I was cast in the school production of Annie. I found others that I could be myself around and I have fond memories from the months we spent together rehearsing and performing. One night, along with a few others from the cast, we had obviously been too engrossed and walked off stage mid-freeze frame. Once we realised we were needed on stage and cackled to ourselves, we slowly shuffled back on stage in the hopes that we hadn't been seen, but of course we had!

Because of the challenges I was facing both inside and outside of school, I couldn't wait to leave. Five years certainly took their time to pass by, but eventually the time had come to think about my future and where I saw myself. The truth was that I had no clue about what my next steps would be. The end of my GCSEs rolled around and, several months later in August 2002 I received my results. My grades were OK – not amazing, but I hadn't done too badly. I spent the summer not knowing what I would do come September, but when it did arrive I had made no firm decision. Sixth form had already started and, following a chat with Jo, I started a Leisure and Tourism course. However a month or so in, I realised my heart wasn't truly invested. I spoke with the Head of Sixth Form, fully expecting her to try and convince me to stay. Instead she gave me the best advice: "Sam, some people are natural studiers; others prefer to start work and earn their own money. Do what you want to do". I so appreciated her honesty and I immediately knew then that I wanted to start my working life at 16

.

I spent six or so months flitting between jobs, not really knowing what to do. None of the jobs captured my attention. After speaking with Jo's mum, Jane, she helped to secure an interview for a full-time position on the checkouts at Sainsbury's. I already had some retail experience following a two-week work experience placement at a pet shop, following which I had been offered a part-time job at the weekend. Working from a young age gave me lots of experience to draw upon in my interview. I got the job and, following my initial training, I set to work within a few weeks. It wasn't the best paid job, but it would give me a regular income and my own money. Over the next year I got to know my colleagues, who were mainly older women. A year later I put in for a transfer over to the food counters and spent almost another year there, before my eyes were drawn to an advert in the free local paper. The advert was for Churchill Insurance, who were seeking operators for their call centre. I had seen the advert before but lacked the confidence to apply. Now I had a few years of work experience under my belt, I applied, as I had nothing to lose by doing so. Within a few weeks I received an invitation to interview, so I made sure I was fully prepared with examples of my work around customer service.

Immediately before my interview I was sat next to someone in the call centre observing them and listening to calls. I was soon fetched and was asked how I found the observation, before multiple competency-based questions. I felt that I answered the questions well but it was now out of my hands. It was during the next week that I received a call to say that I had been successful and, if accepted, I would be placed on the next induction. I gladly accepted and following their vetting process, I was scheduled to start on Monday 5th January 2005.

I resigned from Sainsbury's, knowing that this was the right time to move on. I had had an absolute blast for the previous few years but I needed to take a natural step-up on the career ladder and to take this new opportunity. I didn't put any immediate pressure on myself but gave myself a rough timescale of a year or two to gain some office experience.

After my last Christmas working in an extremely busy retail job, January rolled around and it was now time to do something a little different, to see where the journey took me. I remember stepping into the very busy reception of Churchill, being ushered to the side along with many other new recruits – nervously waiting for my name to be called like I was being selected for a sports team. I have always been a people watcher and I found it funny watching all the staff coming in who were watching us. It definitely gave off "first day at school" vibes. Our trainers Matt and Claire introduced themselves and, along with six other new starters, we were told that we would form a new home team, logging new claims for numerous home insurers. Over the next four weeks, two people were "let go" – following our training we were then released into our own academy team for a few months, before then being dispersed onto the existing teams. As there was (and still is) a pub next to the office, we would often be found in the pub at lunch and after work. I definitely spent a lot of my monthly salary in the pub! Over the next 18 months I made solid friends with many of my colleagues and I was glad that I had made the move. I soon received an internal promotion to the insurer's Counter Fraud Unit and spent the next four years learning the ropes; ending up as a Senior Investigator. I really enjoyed my job and learnt many new skills in catching the fraudsters – it always amazed me the extent some would go to for financial gain.

In 2012, I started to seek a new opportunity as there was no further progression in my role. An internal job advertisement caught my eye for a role many wanted, but that rarely became vacant. An Internal Investigator, investigating cases of staff fraud and gross misconduct. Surely staff wouldn't commit such acts? How wrong I was! I applied, was invited to an interview and spent a long time prepping for what I might be asked. The manager interviewing was renowned for their stiff poker face and no-nonsense approach. I fully expected to receive a grilling, which I did. I thought that I had done well but the decision was out of my hands. Several days later, I was called by the manager who asked to meet me. I was super nervous and, in my self-deprecating mind I convinced myself that it wasn't my time. We met and chatted and they asked how I thought I had performed, which I downplayed. I didn't want to appear too keen or desperate! I was hugely shocked when they offered me the job, I couldn't believe it. A job that very few would get to do was now mine.

After some time shadowing another Investigator, I was allocated my own cases to investigate and I was genuinely shocked by what some employees got up to. Some of those employees I knew of and was stunned to learn of their character. As well as learning on the job, I was enrolled on external training, which would enable me to qualify as a Professional Investigator. I really got to grips with it, and it was interesting to see how others treated me, as we were viewed as the internal police. While I was based in Kent, my job covered all of ou r offices and subsidiaries across the UK. We were often called upon at short notice to conduct interviews elsewhere and I loved going to many different places and achieving great results. I had been in post for 18 months and, despite being having been told a pay rise would happen when I was offered the job, it never did. I didn't want to leave because I loved the job, but I also knew my own worth. So when a position came up on a financial crime team, it was a no-brainer to apply.

I was successful with my application and spent a year with the Anti-Money Laundering team. I made a great friend in my manager, Hannah. Plus, as I was sat next to the Director, Wendy, I got to know her well too. I loved the job and learning more about financial crime. Hannah gave me lots of opportunities to increase my knowledge and was always keen to listen to ideas I had. As Hannah allowed me to facilitate some training, I enjoyed training others. I didn't stay long with the AML team, as I was soon swayed by the bright lights of London – getting myself a job within a fraud prevention agency within a training and compliance role in 2015.

This is where I met Kirstie and Claire. I really got to grips with the job and enjoyed the training of our many clients. Kirstie was on my immediate team and we bonded quickly over our sense of humour. Claire joined a few months after me and, while she was not directly on my team, it was from a request for any French speakers to assist me that we started chatting. We got on well right from then. The business went through a restructure, and one evening I chatted at length to the department director, who quite honestly had no clue or understanding of my role. I stressed that I would prefer to focus on training, rather than the compliance aspect, but I was shot down immediately and informed this would never happen. I smelt bullshit when they said this, and so I had a decision to make. Stay in the mixed role or spread my wings into a new role that would be solely focused on training. I knew my worth, so I made the decision to leave. It wasn't long before Kirstie placed a job advert under my nose for a training role. I eagerly applied and found myself in the interview room a few weeks later, training several people on how to make and fly aeroplanes. Random, but fun! I was offered the job and in a few months found myself settling into my new surroundings. I soon heard that my old team had been split in two, something I had said should happen.

My new training role was a busy and noisy environment and, as someone new, I felt like an outsider for a long time. Sadly, a reshuffle was announced about six months in, which placed hundreds of jobs at risk, including mine. As I was the last in, I was certain I would lose my job, so I started actively pursuing a new job. I soon spotted an ad for an Investigator which involved being out on the road and working from home. This wasn't something I was experienced in, but felt my work history and qualifications perfectly aligned to. I knew there would be hundreds of applicants, but I knew I had to at least try.

I was pleased when I was shortlisted for interview. I nervously waited in reception with all examples of my work whizzing around my mind. Jane introduced herself, along with Ray and we spent the next hour discussing my work history – there was something about them both that put me completely at ease. Jane said that she liked me and that I would hear very soon. I had never had that reaction before and it took me by surprise. True to her word, I was called a few days later and offered the job. I've now been here since 2017 and I have loved every minute of it. While Jane has since retired, we keep in touch and she really is one of the best managers I have worked with. She helped many of the team through personal challenges. As I said, she was the first person I shared my diagnosis with and helped me get through those tough days.

# Chapter 8: Coming Out

I had a very happy childhood and was able to express myself freely. Growing up in the 1990s was great, if not the best decade to live through: it was the last generation before mobile phones, the internet and social media. I was a Spice Girls fan from the start and still am. Being a 90s kid was great and they were the happiest times! Throughout my primary schooling I had playground "romances" but, looking back, I realise they were reflective of my close relationships with females. Most of my friends are female and I've never really felt like "one of the boys". I knew something about me felt different, but I didn't know what this meant at the time. There were no programmes, films or people that I saw at this time that I felt I could relate to in an attempt to understand why I felt different.

It wasn't until I hit the age of 11 and beyond that I was able to start trying to comprehend my thoughts and emotions. Around the late 90s and early 2000s I began to see people like me in the media and press, but I was still having to find out what this meant for me. It was programmes like Graham Norton and *Queer As Folk* along with gay musicians that made me realise why I felt as I did. I found a solid friend in Jo and she was the person that I needed to guide me through those difficult years. As I said, I was subjected to daily taunts of "gay boy" or called a "poof" and "faggot". As much as I tried to show that these had no effect, the words hurt and so I hid a lot of myself as I tried to protect myself against my bullies. Outside of school, Jo and I spent lots of time together and it was around the age of 12 that I confided in her that I had realised I found the same sex attractive. She never told anyone and I knew that she was my safe place. Over the weeks, months and years, our friendship blossomed and we started venturing out on some weekends into London. We were both streetwise for our age and London was a city where everything and anything happened. It was full of an eclectic mix of people and I felt comfortable there. We would go to Soho; it was somewhere we both felt safe. Being able to freely be myself with Jo was great. I could say anything to her, knowing it would go no further.

I spent a lot of time with Jo and her family. It was quite common for us to visit places like Brighton where we would stay for the weekend. We would wander down to the pier and around the shops, and we would spend evenings enjoying the nightlife too. On one of my first visits we watched a drag show before being hauled up on stage to sing-a-long to S Club 7's absolute banger "Reach". Apparently I hogged the microphone, but I don't recall that! We would try to visit for their annual Pride celebrations and it made for a great weekend away. It was a huge comfort to experience the Pride celebrations and to be accepted by the community.

As a teenager, I had very few people I could confide in, other than Jo, and as I couldn't understand what these feelings and emotions meant, I knew I needed to tell someone else. I knew only of one person within my cadet group who was openly gay and who was older than me. I thought they would be able to support or guide me. I plucked up the courage to reach out to them, I sent a text explaining how I had felt for many years and asking if they could give me any advice about coming out and how to understand why I felt like I did. They never gave me any advice and brushed me aside... which I considered quite strange. I thought they too would have navigated the path before me and could offer some pearls of wisdom. I later learnt that they had gone behind my back, "outed" me to somebody and made an insensitive joke. What an arsehole.

I have had a good relationship with my parents and I'm pretty sure they were aware of my personal circumstances at a young age. I never lied to them about my sexuality but, at the same time, I never openly spoke about it. I would stay at Jo's most weekends and around 15 years old, Dad arranged to pick me up. I sat in the front passenger seat as we made our way home. "I want to ask you something", he said. I was fully expecting to be bollocked about why my room was a mess or something about school. Nothing prepared me for what he was about to ask. "Are you gay?"

I took a long pause as my inner voice kicked in as I battled with how to respond. Dad is not silly and is pretty switched on, so I knew I had to take this opportunity to be truthful with him. I took a few moments to compose myself before answering. "Yes. Yes I am". There, I had said it. Years of worry and confusion had built up to the moment that I came out. I felt a sense of panic, as I didn't know how Dad would respond, fully expecting him to react negatively. He was so composed in his response and I will always respect that. We spoke about how I will always be his son and that nothing would be gained from screaming and shouting for me to change. He said the road ahead wouldn't be easy but they would always be my parents. I am lucky to have them, as not everybody has the same support. Coming out also made my bond with Becky even tighter and, despite having our highs and lows over the years as siblings, we remain as strong as ever.

While driving home we continued to chat and agreed he would let Mum know and that we wouldn't let my grandparents know. We didn't think they would understand and thought they would have difficulty in accepting it. They would occasionally ask about girlfriends throughout my teens, but they never questioned me any further. I wish now that they had known so they could see the life I have had, I think they'd be proud.

I kept my coming out private for the rest of my time at Darrick Wood, I confided in only a small handful of friends and I knew it wouldn't be long until those days were behind me. It wasn't until I started full time work at Sainsbury's that I felt that I could be myself without fear of retaliation or worrying what others would think of me. I soon became more sociable and felt comfortable in the presence of others. It was a time that allowed me to be myself and I made friends with my colleagues. Being accepted for being me felt like I had won the jackpot. There were some senior managers who were homophobic; I could tell from their derogatory comments and how they were fearful in approaching me. Jo's mum, Jane, who was my manager at Sainsbury's had seen me grow from a young boy into a man. Her no-nonsense approach and acceptance of who I was helped me to be comfortable with my identity. One Christmas, Jane allowed all counter staff to dress up to inject some fun into our working day and gave me a pink cowboy hat to wear. A senior manager saw me wearing it... and the look of disgust was as if I had slapped a wet fish across his face. He pulled Jane aside demanding that I remove it. Thankfully times have moved on since then, but there are people like that manager who despise our existence. I have learnt to try not to let the opinions of others bother me, and for the most part this works.

As I would go on to learn later in life, acceptance was their problem and not mine. It was around 18 when I briefly dated someone who had been introduced to me through a friend. Whilst the relationship didn't last long, it was the first time that my feelings for a man had felt right.

I would go on to have a bad experience which opened my eyes to how others could take advantage. I met Kenny in an online chat room when I was 19 and his profile said he was a similar age to me. Our profiles had our photos on so we could see what each other looked like, all pretty normal. We began chatting briefly and soon chatted most days as we got on well, having plenty to talk about. After several weeks we swapped mobile numbers and continued chatting over text for the next few weeks. We got on well and never ran out of conversation, so things progressed and we agreed to chat on the phone. Nothing at this point gave me cause for concern. By now a few months had passed and we had built up a connection, albeit online. As we were not local to each other, the topic of conversation moved onto perhaps meeting each other. Kenny seemed a little nervous about it but I thought that was normal. I was also nervous having never done this before. I offered some potential dates which we agreed on but he cancelled a few days befor ehand.

Naively, I thought nothing of this and this happened a few more times before I told him we were either going to meet or not. I knew no better at this age, so we agreed on a final date. On the day, I woke up to a message from him in which he apologised, as he had not been entirely honest with me. He explained that he was not the person I thought he was and that he had lied about many things. I was beyond mad and called him. He avoided my call so it went to voicemail. I eventually heard from him several hours later and demanded that he reveal his true identity. He resisted at first but, later that day, I received his photo, my stomach flipped. Kenny was not 19. He was at least in his 40s. I felt sick to my stomach having felt like I had got to know him. He attempted to chat with me but I walked away right there and then. It was a valuable life lesson about the dangers about the internet. You do not know these people.

It wasn't until moving into my newfound insurance career that I began dating, and what an experience that was. To my disappointment it was nothing like the movies made it out to be! I met some nice guys but, for one reason or another, there wasn't a significant attraction. Meeting new people awakened me to the many different people and personalities, as I would start to discover. I met some timewasters and also guys who struggled with being able to hold a conversation longer than five minutes. There were also those who wanted to get in your pants; that certainly wasn't me. However, meeting others and having mixed experiences meant I started to realise the people I liked.

In my early twenties I met Matt (not his real name). He was a true gentleman and swept me off my feet; everyone who met him thought he was marvelous; nobody said a bad word about him. We had a great relationship for the first year and everything was perfect. However I started to pick up on strange behaviours and noticed awkwardness in some situations. Maintaining my poker face, I kept seeing these red flags and so felt I needed to investigate further. They say to always trust your instinct and I did exactly that. Over a few months my concerns continued to grow. With a little detective work I rumbled his secret. He had been meeting his ex, in work, for some "extra curricular activities". I confronted him early one morning, which is one of a few times in my life that a red mist descended upon me. He knew he had been caught and couldn't lie his way out of it; the photographs and messages were all I needed to see. We stupidly tried to make things work for a few months after that... but once again I caught him out, this time on an app. I ended it, walking away knowing I needed to do this for me. It was the hardest thing to do, but another lesson learnt. Trust your instinct.

I hit rock bottom soon after; I'd been through a person abusing my trust and someone who happily lied to my face. It took a long time to heal and move forward with life. I questioned a lot but, thanks to the support of my friends, they lifted me up in my own time. When trust has been abused, it can be difficult to open up, which is something that has recurred years later. In time, I began dating again but this time I was super aware of those who wanted to play games or who I felt were not being honest. It didn't take much to spot them, but I certainly wasn't being taken for a fool. After a few years, I realised I had met the wrong people and decided that rather than perhaps looking, allow myself to just let things be. If it wasn't meant to be, then so be it.

Summer 2013 arrived and life was in a good place. I felt the most settled I had in a long time. I had spent the last few years looking after myself and allowing time to heal. It was around early July that I received a message on an app from James. He introduced himself and asked how I was. We exchanged messages over the next few days and he seemed nice. I was certainly cautious of him but he was friendly and chatty. It felt odd to not be asked the same set of questions or sent images of body parts. Instead we had good conversations about daily life and of course started getting to know each other. It was hard to gauge what was being said and whether it would change soon, but we kept on messaging and sharing snippets of our life with each other. It felt as though we found each other interesting and our conversation never stopped flowing. James asked if I would like to meet him for a drink. I agreed and we made plans to meet at 8pm in Henry's bar, in Br omley.

# Chapter 9: The Love Story

I had some pre-date nerves but I didn't want to put unnecessary pressure on us meeting. I had met many interesting characters along the way and so I was pretty relaxed about meeting James. I had got caught in some traffic so ended up being slightly late, not getting to Henry's until 8:04pm. You may think the timing insignificant but I'll explain more later. I found James easy to chat with and, when I learned that he worked within theatre, we had lots to chat about. The hours flew by and before we knew it, the bar was closing around midnight. I drove James home and we both said that we enjoyed our night. After a midnight kiss, I drove home with a smile on my face. I glanced at my phone as I got into bed and we swapped numbers, with James asking for a second date.

We saw each other several more times that week. We had a date in London finished by a meal on the South Bank, and then on our third date James cooked a meal of chicken and broccoli bake (which is still one of my favourite meals to have) and a white chocolate and amaretto cheesecake. I really enjoyed his company and we continued to try and see each other often. James then planned a date night at The O2, where we had cocktails at Las Iguanas. We had a lovely chat about the time we had spent together and we then became "official"! The next few months we spent lots of time together and enjoyed both time at James' flat and days out. We made plans for a long weekend in Chagford and had a great time away... and I knew that I wanted to continue what we had. September 2013 arrived and I was ready for my Best Man duties at Jo's brother's wedding. I invited James to the evening reception and knew it felt right to introduce him to my parents, Becky and my friends. The day went without a hitch and everyone liked him.

Before long, Christmas was fast approaching – as self-confessed Christmas lovers, we planned lots and were excited for the festive season ahead. As we decorated the Christmas tree on 1st December 2013 and watching a festive film, James turned to me and said "I love you". I instantly said it back. I had never been happier. In 2014, we planned our first holiday together and we jetted off to Mauritius which is the most beautiful island to visit. The white sandy beaches and crystal clear water were just perfection. Upon returning home we spoke about our future and spoke about moving in together. James soon sold his flat and, in late 2014, we moved into a beautiful cottage in Crockenhill, Kent.

We loved making the house; it was such a joy to have our own space to make our own. The following year, while staying at the Ashdown Forest Country Club Hotel, in the confines of a secret garden, James proposed with a Haribo ring. I had never expected it, but of course I said "yes". A year later, on 24th July 2016, exactly three years from the date we met, we got married at Buxted Park Hotel, Uckfield. It was a magical day and it really was the best day. Our first dance to The Carpenters' "You're The One" was timed to start at 8:04pm, the exact time that we had met.

Our family grew in April 2017 when we welcomed our beautiful dachshund Ralph into our lives. He is the craziest but most loveable bundle of joy. He is my shadow and is never far from me, wherever I am. He has picked up on the changes over the last few years and has become fiercely protective of me. It has got to the point now where he doesn't go to bed until I am in bed.

James and I travelled well before M came home, and have holidayed in Antigua, St Lucia, the Dominican Republic, Cape Verde, Mexico and Greece. We did go on a Disney Cruise several years ago too, which was an amazing experience.

We may not be able to travel internationally now, due to the progression of my symptoms but hopefully can holiday a little closer to home. With MND, we have learnt to live life one day at a time.

# Chapter 10: Relationships

What do you say to someone who is living with a life-limiting illness? "Hi, how are you?" is probably a good place to start. I say this because, even three years on I can see the apprehension in others about how to approach me. That's not to say it's a bad thing, I have found myself in the same scenario, perplexed about what to say.

In the days following my diagnosis, people would often look at me blankly, not knowing what to say, frightened they would hurt or upset me. Nobody did ever upset me, I just appreciated being able to have a chat and to be as normal as possible. I received many messages of support and love and these really got me through. Sharing myself so publicly meant I didn't have to keep repeating myself. I admire and thank those who did reach out and allowed me the space to offload. The truth is that I know I would struggle to know what to say to someone in my position then and now. My advice is to carry on, allow the conversation to flow or be a shoulder to cry on. If the person wants to talk about their illness, let them. You can ask if they're comfortable talking about it. I have never wanted to be treated differently because of MND and so I gravitate towards routine and normality as much as I can. I often get, "Can I ask you a question?" I simply respond with "Absolutely. I have been asked every question imaginable, so go ahead".

This puts them at ease and gives them permission to ask whatever they like. I would much rather the person took something away from our interaction and learnt about MND, rather than not asking at all. I remain happy and upbeat, but not everyone will and that's OK.

I occasionally encounter people who... let's just say... believe they have superpowers. One such individual approached me in Charing Cross Station while I was with my sister and cousin after an indulgent afternoon tea. I was still walking then, with the support of my walking stick. I spotted this middle-aged man who kept staring at me – I presume because of my good looks. I glanced back and he didn't break his stare. He approached me and, with absolutely no tact or grace, asked "So why have you got a walking stick?" Wowzer, this dude had more front than Brighton Pier. "I have MND, it affects my legs and how I walk". He said that he would pray for me, which I was quite comforted by as he wouldn't be the first to do so. In his hand he was holding a long thin stick. Following his offer of prayer he stood back several paces and began waving and pointing said stick at me. That's right, he was either casting a magic/voodoo spell or the modern day miracle worker had revealed his true identity. My cousin and sister, exchanging looks of disbelief, started to remove themselves, walking away. "I cure you of your illness," he said. Sadly, I awoke the very next day and I hadn't been. Bugger.

MND not only affects the body, it also spills over into all areas of life. I like to think that I try not to let it consume every part of me. My personality may have slightly changed as my humour and wit may have darkened, but I am still Sam. I am not, and never will be, my diagnosis. MND has done equally great but horrific things to every relationship

I have. As much as I wanted my relationships to remain as they were, a life-changing diagnosis is likely to have an effect on everyone. As much as it feels weird to say that, I would question why a relationship hadn't changed after such a significant life event. So, yes. Every relationship changed. Some for better, and sadly some for worse.

I see MND like me being at the epicentre of an earthquake. The shockwaves are felt by those connected to me. I may be the person living with it, but it has affected all of those around me.

Over the last three years I have built and found a community of MND friends who have enriched my life in many ways. Not only are some of these people living with a life-limiting illness, but there are also the amazing people who love, care and support them. I count myself as part of this community that embraces those newly diagnosed and uplifts others when the days are dark. However, what hurts most is when we lose a fellow warrior. I have now lost more than several people in the last six months, and their losses hit me hard. Losing them reminds me that my own mortality awaits me, and this keeps my mind focused on what I still want to accomplish. While my relationships with the community are fairly recent, I often engage with them more than my family and close friends. They truly understand what it is like to journey the same path, despite having our own unique stories. The MND community are a supportive crowd, but I have learnt to not make my entire existence about MND. It just so happens to be part of my life, and not the reason for living. I have gone on to set up my own Facebook community "My MND Mates" – a supportive place for those diagnosed in the younger generations, but welcome to all.

As our lives naturally evolve, so do the relationships throughout our entire lives. My circle of friends when we were leaving school was large. My mum said to me when I was leaving secondary school to be mindful about saying how we would all stay in touch. I thought this was rather an odd thing to say, but true to her word I saw that over the next few decades my friendship circle quickly shrank. I was fine with that. I was never the popular kid and never wanted to be. I am at a point in life now where my friendship circle remains small and that's good for me. As my life changed in my teens, 20s and 30s, the people around me changed. I would go on to make friendships with others that I had met or worked with briefly, and they still remain my friends years later. I have lost friends too, some naturally because our lives drifted apart and some because of disagreements or other reasons.

My illness has changed all of my relationships. I have become closer to some because of my dependency on them and this has given us the opportunity to have moments we would not have shared before. It has also enabled me to rekindle relationships with others years later, and I am so pleased this happened. I have learnt about what does and doesn't matter and to not hold grudges, as well as letting go of things that do not uplift me. All of that left my life in March 2022.

Some relationships survived and some didn't. I have lost friends in different ways, I've been lied to, among other things. I'm never going to know why, but if they're reading this – hey, I see you! Then there are relationships that have shown up in every way possible. These have really surprised me and I am so thankful that our friendship has blossomed and to have you in my life. I learnt who and what matters, the most powerful of life lessons to learn.

I have gone on to forge new friendships that I never saw coming, one of those being the lovely Esther. Esther works for the Motor Neurone Disease Association as a Community Fundraiser; however, she is so much more than that. You'll recall my hesitation in wanting to engage with the association in the weeks and months post-diagnosis until an email popped up in my inbox. It was an email from Esther introducing herself. There was absolutely no pressure to engage with her other than a hand of support with an open offer of conversation. I mulled over her email and realised her approach was comforting, so several days later I replied and we scheduled a telephone call for the following week.

In all honesty, I didn't know what to expect, but Esther allowed me the space and time to share my story in my way. I speak with Esther every few months and we have kept in touch – my time with her is cherished and deeply appreciated. She has always approached me with cotton wool gloves, lending a listening ear when I have needed to offload. She has also been working hard in helping me work through my bucket list.

---

## Esther

Looking at the MND Association Twitter account (when it was still called that!), the first glimpse I caught of Sam was his beaming smile, alongside his husband James, on his post about his diagnosis and GoFundMe page link:

*"We all die. The goal isn't to live forever; the goal is to create something that will."*

*How long will I be here?*

*How will my family and friends cope with seeing me deteriorate before their eyes?*

*How will I cope?*

*What will I leave behind?*

Wow! What a moving story he'd written, and here was someone who also liked a challenge – with the goal of raising £50,000 to help families affected by MND!

I loved the bucket list Sam had created and quickly reached out to let him know about our support for him and his family, and how I would love to support him and help with his fundraising.

I was so taken with his way of describing his feelings with such eloquence. The questions he posed on the page seemed to reflect the rush of thoughts that might be difficult to untangle or express after receiving such life-changing news – yet Sam managed to put them into words with amazing clarity. I also saw that he'd recorded a very moving video about his diagnosis and thought how generous he was to let others into his world in this way.

I was delighted when Sam replied and we had our first "cuppa and catch up" later that week.

Since this first chat, I have had a deep respect and admiration for Sam. He has a lovely way about him, down to earth, pragmatic, easy to talk to, funny, and attentive; most notable was the way he has approached this new, uninvited, turn in his life. From what I see, I think he's always had a positive way of framing things, evident through his blog DaddyDad&Me, about fatherhood of an adopted child.

He told me he found writing the blogs cathartic – there's certainly power in putting your thoughts onto paper and then there's the knowledge that you may just help someone else with your words. This is a very heartening thought, especially for someone like Sam, who is a particularly caring soul.

Now, facing the reality of MND, where statistically over 50% of people diagnosed with MND will die within two years of diagnosis, I could sense Sam's approach to life had become steely and focused; He was determined to remain true to himself, with a thoughtful and positive outlook, but now with a new potency to live life to the fullest – and so, his bucket list was born!

I was excited to try to help Sam reach his goals, and also felt his voice could play an influential role in raising awareness of MND within the LGBTQ+ community and show how the disease can affect younger people too.

I recall how blown away Sam was by the support from his friends – a lovely lady was going to put on a ball that summer and another friend was busy bringing to life a special music festival in Bath. It was clear that Sam enjoyed organising the ball and it became a central focus. It was an important opportunity to bring everyone together in solidarity and support in the face of his diagnosis.

I don't usually get the privilege to attend events, but it just worked out beautifully that I was able to be there to support Sam, meeting his lovely family and friends. Such an unforgettable and heartwarming evening, filled with connection and meaning.

I should've guessed there would be some amazing theatrical twists too, with the waiters suddenly bursting into harmonised song! It took everyone by surprise and the room lit up even more.

The love and affection for Sam and James in the room was palpable. Several of their friends spoke with me about how much they loved Sam and shared fundraising ideas they'd like to take on and dedicate in support of Sam and his family.

The practical support and strength of his parents and sister was again very moving to witness, they are such a dynamic family and were already progressing plans to sell up their home and find somewhere they could all live together, so they would be right there on hand for Sam and his family. This was no small undertaking, but they saw this was possible and nothing would stand in their way of making this happen for their Sam.

There's no measure to show just how much all this support means, but I'm certain the ongoing love and encouragement has helped Sam get through the extremely challenging times that are often an unseen, or hidden, part of living with MND.

Since that first event, I've watched how Sam's momentum has continued to grow and evolve. I've been absolutely thrilled to see him become a powerful voice for the MND community through the many campaigns he's led with the MND Association – especially in raising awareness and giving support for those newly diagnosed. And let's not forget the incredible input he had with ITV's *Coronation Street* and its millions of viewers!

As MND started to impact Sam's mobility, Sam has continued with his generous openness to share these struggles through social media.

This is the only way many people will ever glimpse the impact of MND, unless they have experienced it directly in some way. It's this kind of openness that educates and breaks down barriers to understanding and, like all Sam's family and friends, I'm so proud of what he is doing, despite how hard it is.

At the time of writing (27/6/25) Sam has completed 73 of his 100 bucket list wishes – when you see how creative they are, you will understand that this is some achievement! (I was delighted to fix one for Sam, by introducing him to another fundraiser who happened to be a racing driver and drove Sam around Brands Hatch! ... number 74).

There's still lots to do and we're still on the hunt for a connection to the Spice Girls – so please shout if you can help!?!

---

MND has caused a significant strain on mine and James' marriage and has changed us both from the people we were. The roles within our relationship have changed as my needs have increased. James has become a carer, which has blurred the relationship. It is often said that moving house and getting married are the most stressful events to live through. Well, you can add a life-limiting illness to that.

Any chronic illness will place pressure on a relationship, despite you not wanting it to, especially when the role of a carer becomes increasingly demanding. Marriages are pushed to their limits and may come under immense pressure. For some, it is too much and those relationships are broken, whereas other marriages go on to build unbreakable bonds. Marriage is equally beautiful and ugly; it can take a lot from you but also give lots too. The relationship I have with James has naturally evolved and changed over time. I'm not angry about much because of MND, but I hate what it has done to us.

MND has also tested my relationships with family. Living with my parents and sister has naturally had its ups and downs. We have got through some really challenging times, but most of all we've learnt that each of us needs our own space and time. Five adults and a child living under one roof would test anybody. As I am heavily dependable on others, this has meant that we've had to learn and adapt routines. Sometimes we've got it right and other times we failed. It has been a lot for us to learn, it really makes you look at life differently. Priorities change as much as we do as people.

# Chapter 11: Accessibility & Disability

As my diagnosis came early, in terms of my symptoms presenting themselves, to the naked eye it was pretty much a hidden illness. Throughout much of 2022, I had no issues with walking or being mobile. I took M to Costa one weekend for lunch and wasn't particularly confident in my ability to be able to hold a tray with our lunch on. This was my first encounter in which I questioned whether I needed to ask for help. I battled with my mind. Would staff just laugh if I asked for help? What if they said "no"? The lady I asked said "yes"' without hesitation. I still felt as though I needed to explain why I needed to ask, so I said that I had a health issue. I didn't need to do this, but it felt like the right thing to do at the time. I have gone on to learn that you should never need to explain yourself, but it has taken time to learn that.

Living close to London and being a musical theatre fan, I often visit the West End to watch a show. I've been watching them since I was young so have seen hundreds over the last 30 years. James was working on a production at The Menier Chocolate Factory for a few months in 2023 and I went along to the press night. It had rained earlier in the day and it was wet underfoot as I made my way from London

Bridge station. I had never had any issues in London before... but this was the first time I felt uneasy and unstable on my feet; the pavement felt like an ice rink despite my rubber soled trainers. Anyone walking close to me or at speed made me feel deeply anxious. I made sure I positioned myself away from people and walked at a slower pace. This experience was the catalyst for realising my body was changing and that my previously hidden disability was in fact no longer hidden. I made the decision that it was now time to think about the use of a walking ai d.

In my opinion, accessibility is ugly, or at least it can be. A quick Google search for anything mildly assistive in anyway and you soon realise it's likely to be grey, clunky and more often than not stupidly expensive. When I was forced to adjust from able-bodied to disabled, I was damn sure that we were doing it on my terms. I didn't want something ugly, and so my search for attractive walking aids begun. It didn't take me long to discover "Cool Crutches", an independent business run by somebody who fully understood disability. There were crutches and walking sticks in all different colours and designs. Hallelujah! I could have a choice of, leopard print, disco, glow in the dark... you name it, they had it. I went on to choose a black stick decorated with white stars. One of my first outings with it was to the theatre and, as my stick was clearly visible, it gave a clear sign to others. It not only helped to mobilise me, but also most people would move out of my way or let me walk by. The ushers at the Phoenix Theatre were super helpful and their accessibility team had everything sorted, which made for a positive experience. Yes the stick was a sign to others of my disability, but it stood out for the right reasons; it was fun! They are two words rarely seen together, 'fun' and 'disability'... but businesses like Cool Crutches are making that happen.

I used my stick for a long while before transitioning to my wheelchair. The stick had helped support my balance, but as I started to feel a change in my legs and wasn't particularly keen on face-planting the floor, so transitioning to a wheelchair felt like the safer option. The first time I ventured out in my wheelchair I was extremely self-conscious. There was no disguising it, as it is in itself a visible piece of equipment. At first, I felt as though all eyes were on me and it was quite uncomfortable being stared at. Three years on I am still stared at, but I don't pay too much attention to it. I'm never sure if it's because I'm young or if the other person is playing "guess the disability". Nowadays, I think nothing of it because it is part of my everyday life. I now have the confidence to look back, and most will avert their eyes. Although every so often I partake in a game of "stare out". Guess who wins?! (It's not them). Young children often look at me in my wheelchair and I give them a gentle smile back to show that I'm not scary. Their curiosity comes from the fact that they are unlikely to have seen many wheelchair users. I do wonder why others look, and can only think that young wheelchair users are in a very small minority, whereas it is quite common for older generations. The world needs to see people from all walks of life. We can only be seen and heard by being visible, and loud.

Navigating life in a wheelchair has taught me that there is still so much to be done in terms of accessibility. I find myself in a minority that has to fight for change or to have our voices heard. We can be seen as difficult for wanting to change society's perception of disability, but we have to be outspoken to effect that change. I've only learnt this from being disabled and coming up against many barriers.

Being physically sat in my wheelchair shifted my perspective on the outside world. I spend a lot of my time when in my wheelchair surveying the path ahead and observing how others approach me. It is surprising how many paths, kerbs and surfaces are unsuitable or dangerous. I have had many encounters with the above and found myself almost being catapulted out of my chair. Retail spaces are improving and are mindful of consumers with mobility needs; however, there are still huge improvements to be made. Many remain inaccessible because of huge steps into them or being unable to move around. There is one particular clothing store that packs their stores so tightly with stands and the like, that it is impossible to venture much further than a few metres into the store. We challenged one particular store and all the store representative could say was "Yeah, bad isn't it?" Hardly a recipe for positive change to be made. By contrast, in an encounter with Oliver Bonas, a store assistant approached me and asked how I found navigating around their store in my wheelchair. I gave both positive feedback and a few notes, which they said they would feed back to their Head Office. I really appreciated being asked about my experience. These are all things I never had to contemplate before but something I find myself doing on a daily basis. We won't change the world overnight, but every positive change is a step in the right dire ction.

There is an unconscious bias in how the world and society views disability. If being pushed in my wheelchair, I've at times been ignored and overlooked, so someone can speak to whoever is pushing me. It can translate as if being in a wheelchair means "incapable". I surprise others when I start speaking and interacting with them. I had an encounter a few years ago shopping on Regent Street when a sales assistant made the assumption that I wasn't capable of, or had difficulty with, engaging in conversation. It was to her obvious surprise when I spoke, but she continued to exaggerate the pronunciation of every word, speaking abnormally loud as though I was hard of hearing, "I'LL PUT YOUR SHOPPING AT THE COUNTER, OK?" Disability does not mean incapability. We are able, but it means we do things differently.

I miss being able to go out without forward planning, when everything could be spontaneous. However, almost every new journey has to be researched and meticulously planned.

- Are they accessible?
- To what extent?
- Are there any steps?
- Does their website stipulate how accessible they are?
- What does Google Maps show?
- Is disabled parking available?
- What accessible facilities do they have?
- Do they have a lift? (Is it working on the day?)
- Did we need to inform the venue beforehand of accessibility requirements?

The list is endless, depending on where we want to go. There are very few accommodation settings that have truly grasped what accessibility means. We've experienced places that market themselves as such because they have a wet room with grab rails. However, I recently discovered Windmill Barns in Warwickshire and was seriously impressed at their offerings. They genuinely understood the needs of their guests and had hot tubs with hoists. It made for an enjoyable stay and took away a lot of unnecessary worry.

Another barrier to overcome was being fed in public. I was able to manage most things at first, but soon had difficulty in lifting and holding cutlery along with trying to lift up a drink for long enough. I accepted that it was time to be fed by someone else.

I wasn't initially comfortable being fed in public as I needed to adjust to someone assisting me. Feeding myself was something I had done for more than three decades and I was now having to revert to being fed by someone, like when I was a baby. It's only when someone first fed me that I realised I have my own way of eating a meal. We all do. If I was fed and it didn't feel right, I tried to avoid biting the hand that fed me, but failed a few times. Several years on, we've got the routine perfected. Being fed in public is a different experience and it took a while to feel comfortable. At first we looked like the most romantic couple as I was being fed, but on more than a few occasions I have caught a glimpse of another diner staring my way. I get it; being fed as an adult isn't seen as the norm, but it is my normal. If they stare a little too long, a quick glance at them is usually enough to break the gaze. I try not to give much thought or consideration to it, but I'm only human. I've been fed in many different environments and try to take no notice of anyone. I am fed not out of choice but necessity.

I have had mixed experiences at restaurants when in my wheelchair, some are keen to place you at the back, which is often near the toilets, despite there being plenty of seating available elsewhere. I am impressed by businesses that engage with me and aren't afraid to ask what adjustments are needed. The little things mean the most.

I am frustrated when organisations proclaim they are accessible, only to be anything but. Last year I went to a local restaurant that said they had ground floor access for accessibility. However, when we arrived at the door, a six inch step at the door was their ground floor access. The venue thought that because they have a door at ground level, it means they are accessible. I'm afraid not. There is no way a wheelchair would have navigated this and so we had to request the assistance of a staff member to help us. We gave them feedback and will always provide feedback from a point of view of raising awareness. Change can't happen without communicating the issues. I'd actively encourage everyone to spend time in a wheelchair to experience the outside world and the challenges faced on a daily basis. I really do believe many organisations will learn a lot about what they currently offer

.

Nobody tells you that disability carries with it an expensive price tag. While we may get VAT relief for purchasing some products, I often need to buy things because of disability that add to my quality of life, or are needed as part of my daily life. There are also services that have unnecessary barriers that prevent people from accessing services. I recently attempted to obtain an air mover pressure relief cushion but was told this could not be arranged, unless I had an open wound. Prevention is surely better than cure? Clearly not! This is something that I will now buy. The weird thing here is that an open wound will cost the NHS far more than the cost of the cushion...

There are very few "perks" that come with disability and so you have to take what you can to make the most out of life. Here are my recommendations and some of the things I have found helpful that will hopefully save you some money: Most are UK-based, so, if you are based outside of the UK, take a look for similar schemes near you.

## Access card

The card is awarded to you based upon the level of support and assistance required. Many venues accept the card and this negates the need to have to constantly explain yourself. Lots of ticketing platforms accept the card, making the process easier (but you'll still need to wait in the annoying online queues!)

## APCOA parking

They are the owner of all SouthEastern trains car parks in the UK. You ca apply for a yearly permit online, which grants you free parking at all of their car parks. We've saved hundreds of pounds using this.

## Blue badge – disabled parking

It took an age to sort (six months) but it has been so useful to have. They're obtained from your local council, who will ask for evidence of your disability. Apply as soon as you can, but be prepared for a long wait.

### Cinema Exhibitors' Association (CEA) card

A handy card to have for cinema lovers. You'll need to apply and pay £10 every year. Dependent on the cinema, you pay full price and your companion goes free. We've used this alongside our cinema's loyalty scheme and paid less than £10 for two tickets.

### Hidden Disability Sunflower

This visible lanyard allows others to be mindful of a hidden disability; as such this would be useful to have, especially when symptoms are not immediately obvious.

### Nike "Flyease"

I was having difficulty with footwear; if my laces came undone, I would have difficulty in tying them on my own. Nike designed their Flyease range with input from the disabled community. They are entirely hands-free to put on and remove, and they are nice to look at too. Other brands, take note!

### Personal Independence Payment (PIP)

This was previously known as Disability Benefit and is paid weekly. Living with a disability comes at a cost, as there will be things you need to purchase to assist and support you; this benefit is there for that.

Apply as soon as you can; any payments will be backdated to when the claim was received. You will be assessed and scored in two parts, mobility and daily living. You need to provide them with evidence of your disability.

## Theatre accessibility schemes

Most theatres have their own access schemes to make it as accessible as possible for all to experience live theatre. I have watched many shows at a fraction of the cost. I was able to see *Moulin Rouge* from the second row of the dress circle for less than £60 for two seats. The seats next to us were being sold at more than £100 each!

# Chapter 12: Carers

If anyone had said to me five years ago, when life was good, that I would have to introduce carers into my life, I would have laughed in your face in disbelief. Even the notion of being butt naked in front of anyone other than my husband would have made me seriously uncomfortable! But this was the very road I was about to travel on and little did I know about what was to come.

In 2022, I was able to do more or less everything myself. Over time, I began to notice that simple things like showering or getting dressed would become more tiring. This is where I learnt the art of adaptation. I tried to find different ways of getting things done. In what felt like no time at all, I found it difficult to lift my arms up to my head and climbing in and out of the bath to shower was not only difficult, but also dangerous. This was the risk I was willing to take to keep control of my life. I soon found inventive ways to dress myself and brush my teeth, which I thought were pretty original. However, they would only work for a while before I had to adapt and find a new normal as the body kept on changing.

Thankfully, once the house move went through, I could live entirely on the ground floor and, because our en-suite was a wet room, it made showering much safer. However because of the distance we had moved, it meant much of my care team had to change. It took months for this to happen but, after having a chat with my Occupational Therapist, it was agreed that now would be the time to consider employing carers for my ever-increasing needs.

Having to contemplate this was in itself a challenge to overcome. I had to keep reminding myself of why this was now happening, but it still didn't make the transition any easier. A social worker visited me at home to undertake an assessment of my needs and I remembered the advice once given to me; provide them with an overview of what a bad day looks like. The assessment lasted several hours and covered every aspect of my life: washing, dressing, independence, hobbies, cooking and so on. You name it, everything was discussed.

The Social Worker informed me that she believed I would be eligible for council funding but, as she would need to present my case to a panel for approval, she didn't know how long it would take. As the meeting came to a conclusion we exchanged pleasantries but, just as she left the room, she asked if she could shake my hand. I had just spent the last two hours explaining my lack of mobility and it felt like this had fallen on deaf ears. This really didn't give me much confidence, but I reminded her of my disability as I watched her face flush with embarrassment.

It took months for my funding to be approved and, as with any council, I had to provide evidence of incoming and outgoing funds; again this felt like another hurdle to navigate because, if you had too much money, they'd expect you to contribute to funding your own care, which in my eyes is wrong.

Once the funding of one hour of care was approved I wasn't given any information about care agencies to approach. A quick Google search returned hundreds of results and it soon became a minefield of information which was overwhelming. All that I could do was to look at online reviews, but even they weren't particularly helpful. I emailed my MND Coordinator Kelly, who was able to give me the name of two agencies who I made contact with. The first I telephoned and spoke with an honest man who explained that, while they couldn't offer me any care, the council were "taking the piss by only offering an hour of care every day". This was useful to know as he asked what I did for lunch and dinner, saying that it should not fall to my family to do this. At an absolute minimum I should have three care calls a day. I contacted the second agency, Caremark, who arranged for a supervisor to visit me at home and to chat through my care requirements in a few days' time.

It's only when someone asked about my morning routine that I realised I never paid much attention to it but that I did everything out of habit. I really had to think about what I did. I had got to the point with showering every few days, mainly due to time constraints as I was dependent on somebody washing me. I'd also had a handful of toileting accidents and this made the employment of carers all the more important. I chatted through my beauty regime and everything was documented to ensure all ran smoothly. I was then asked what type of carer I wanted. It genuinely threw me, as I hadn't given any thought and that I would have a choice. After some thought, I explained that I would prefer carers older than me, as I might feel awkward with somebody younger. My choices were noted and care calls were scheduled to start the following week in July 2024. Weirdly enough, my care team are all younger than me, and it's never been a problem.

I won't lie but I was really apprehensive about getting naked in front of total strangers. I had experienced enough embarrassment letting Mum shower me once while letting it all hang out. So, I tried to prepare myself for what was to come. My first care call came and Kirsty immediately put my mind at ease. Weirdly, I gave no thought to it as she showered me; she joked that she had seen so many bodies of all shapes and sizes that she was quite oblivious to it. Over the next few weeks, the remainder of my care team were introduced to me. I soon got to know them and their personalities, as they are all quite different to each other. I soon noticed after a few weeks the positive effects of showering every day. Never underestimate the power of a shower!

I ended up complaining to the council because the funding awarded didn't cover the cost of my carers. I gained the impression that they were trying to pay as little as possible. This ended up being escalated to their Director of Social Care who soon realised they had no argument when I told him I had been given no information about care agencies to approach. They ended up agreeing to additional funding, and I hope a lesson was learnt in that they cannot expect people to know if they aren't provided with the right information. This was all new to me and we can only go from the information provided to us. It is the same with disability, we don't know what we don't know.

Several months later, I noticed a dip in my mental health and I couldn't pinpoint why. I felt pretty upbeat but something felt different, and it took a while for me to understand why. With carers now being part of my everyday life, I realised there was no going back from this, and they would be part of my life until the very end. With many things I just accepted them for what they were, but while having carers was a positive, I realised how much had changed in such a short amount of time. It was a reminder that MND is relentless and continues to take all the time. It blurred the lines of how I saw myself and how the world saw me. I lost a piece of me for a while as I adjusted.

I'll soon be approaching a year with carers (July 2025) and the team (Adeep, Dani, Kirsty, Martha and Vishnu) have become part of the family; weirdly, it feels like they have always been here. They each have their own ways of doing things and I like the variety in how they do things. My initial reservations about getting naked in front of total strangers is no more. It's funny how comfortable I am with it now; I don't bat an eyelid.

My care needs have evolved over time due to the nature of the disease as it progresses. Having started with one care call a day, and following a review from the council, I now have three care calls. The morning call is to shower and dress me, then a lunchtime call to prepare and feed me lunch. I then finish with a bedtime call. I recently (April 2025) requested another care review by the council as the time needs to be increased but this will not be a quick process, and there will be unnecessary hoops to jump through. I will end up needing high-level care and my needs will continually evolve. I know that this is what life will look like. As I still work full-time, this can make for a very busy day but the normality is something that I need and enjoy. I often joke that I don't have time to have MND.

# Chapter 13: Technology

Would you believe me if I said that I have written this book using only my head control mouse on my MacBook? Well I have done exactly that! Thanks to advances in technology, I am able to utilise the free software provided by Apple that enables me to still use my laptop, albeit in a different way.

The in-built camera tracks my head movements and the mouse moves in the same direction. I use the on-screen keyboard to type and the camera watches my facial features to perform certain tasks, which can be amended by me. To click or select something I move the mouse to where I need it and then smile, which performs the click function. I select and copy by scrunching my nose and moving the mouse before clicking. Other functions can be used by raising eyebrows or sticking my tongue out. It really is a clever piece of kit that allows me to maintain independence while living with a disability. The same software is available on iPads and iPhones. This technology isn't available on all mobiles and tablets, and this should swiftly change so that this level of accessibility is standard.

One of the first things I was recommended to complete by the MND Association was to bank my voice. MND can take away the ability to speak completely, or it can alter the voice, meaning it may not sound like it once did. I feel lucky that three years on I can still speak, although my voice has changed. Thanks to Speak Unique, I banked my voice, which is saved digitally for whenever I need to use it. The way in which the voice is banked comes from recording the voice by reading a book titled "I Will Always Be Me". I struggled to read the book because I kept crying as I read it aloud. However I did eventually manage to record it and my digital voice was ready within a few days. The software enables users to have a digital voice that sounds similar to their own. I have the app all ready and waiting for as and when I need it. The typical rite of passage was to test it to see how swear words would sound! A recent update for iPhone users also gives them the opportunity to record their voice.

Emily, my Occupational Therapist put me in contact with Environmental Control, for which I thank her. I fully expected a rodent extermination service to arrive... and was most disappointed when it didn't. This service exists to assess your needs (environment) and any aids that will support your daily life. They consider such things as personal alert alarms and assistive technology. The officer who assessed my needs spoke with me at length about daily life and referred me to other services, as well as giving me lots of useful information. At the time of her visit I found it very challenging to hold and use my iPhone. She said "You do realise that you can operate your phone using voice or head control?" My response, "WHAT?!" clearly startled her. She showed me exactly how to set it up there and then. The software is available on iPhones, iPads and MacBooks under the Accessibility setting. I use voice control, which gives every selectable field a number. Once the number is selected it picks that particular field, and so on. I have used my phone entirely hands-free for a long while and it changed my life. I can operate my phone and do all the things I could do before. Once I'm in bed I can even scroll for hours on TikTok!

One of the two services I was referred to was for a "Lifeline" alarm. I was given a wrist device that would trigger an alarm in the house if I fell. I can also press a button on the watch, which triggers the alarm. When I can no longer use my arms, I have a click button I can operate using my foot.

The second service was to be provided with a head mouse and foot clicker buttons for using my work laptop. As I wear glasses for work, a small reflective silver sticker dot is positioned on the nose bridge. The camera positioned on the laptop picks up the sticker and moves according to how the sticker moves. I am still able to use my mouse but, due to loss of motor function, clicking the mouse has become increasingly difficult. I have left and right foot buttons which are plugged into the head mouse – I use these rather than clicking the mouse itself. This is helping me now, and will enable me to carry on working for as long as possible.

Following the wet room renovation, we had a wet and dry toilet installed. This marvellous but costly piece of equipment has enabled me to regain some independence and dignity. I am able to operate it by myself. Once I have done what I need to do, I pop my foot on the foot button and a powerful jet of hot water washes me. Once I remove my foot, the jet stops and the toilet flushes. I am then dried for several minutes with a continual flow of warm air. This is by far my favourite gadget!

There is also a full length body air dryer that I use by standing in front of; it dries me from top to toe. It also means I don't need a towel to be dried.

I also have a machine that feeds me my meals, called Obi. The meal is divided into the four sections and the machine switched on. I have two buttons on the floor which operate the robotic arm, which has a spoon at the end. I click one button, which scoops from the section and moves the spoon to my mouth. A second click returns the spoon to the same section and completes the next scoop. A click of the next button moves the spoon to the next section. It is another great piece of equipment that allows me to regain some independence.

I have always enjoyed taking photos and videos but, as the disease progressed, I stopped capturing them as I couldn't lift my phone. I saw that Rayban sold eyewear which can be operated hands-free. They come with a hefty price tag of £300+ but, in my eyes (pardon the pun), they are worth it. Not only can I take images and videos but the built-in speakers also allow me to listen to music from my phone, and make and receive calls in addition to live streaming. Software updates continue to enhance their functionality. Mine also automatically darken in lighter conditions, so they can be dual purpose.

An amazing piece of technology available to those living with MND is EyeGaze. This is technology on a tablet that tracks eye movements, which can be used to operate software, which means we can still communicate without our voices or mobility of limbs.

Finally I have to tell you about the technology I have on my electric wheelchair. The wheelchair is able to be controlled solely by me, but comes with two settings which are another improvement to quality of life. The first is the ability to tilt the chair to an almost horizontal position, which allows me to redistribute the pressure from sitting for long periods of time. The other function is being able to raise the seat. This is perfect for social occasions; it means I can put myself at head height meaning I don't need to strain my neck.

These advances in technology support those living with life-limiting illnesses such as MND and enable us to retain independence and a quality of life. I shudder to think how different life would be without those advances in technology.

# Chapter 14: The Unexpected Hospital Stay

Despite visiting hospitals every few months, I aim to get in and out as swiftly as possible. I do not like them and try to avoid them if I can. On Christmas Eve, 2024 I encountered a pain in my lower abdomen that I had never felt before. The pain intensified over several hours and I ended up going to Accident and Emergency in the early hours. After numerous examinations and tests, they diagnosed a urinary tract infection. I was sent on my way with some antibiotics and I was back to normal in no time.

Many of us living with MND do not drink copious amounts of fluids because that means repeated trips to the toilet. When you're already exhausted from just living with the illness, the thought of venturing to the toilet multiple times a day would wipe me out. However not drinking plentiful fluids increases the risk of infections. It's a double-edged sword having to constantly weigh up what to do.

Despite trying to be more conscious of drinking more, on Mother's Day 2025 I started to experience the same pain I had felt several months earlier. I tried to ignore it but the pain worsened quickly. Mum and Dad ended up taking me to hospital, where I explained my symptoms to the nurse, and said that I thought it was an infection like before. She examined me in my wheelchair and we were directed to another area where we were to be seen by a doctor.

The room we were in was heated to the same temperature as the surface of the sun. It was mightily uncomfortable as we sat there sweating. An hour or so passed before I was eventually called in by the doctor, who clearly wasn't happy about working the nightshift. His attitude stank from the outset and he was certainly not in the mood. I once again explained my symptoms and the pain I was in. "Why are you in a wheelchair?" he asked without any compassion. I could tell this wasn't going to be a positive experience. "I have MND and I find i t difficult to walk. I still use my legs but I'm very wobbly." I said. He was clearly confused by my explanation, as he asked if I would be able to get on the bed to be examined. I said it would be extremely difficult and that others had no problem with me sitting in my wheelchair as they examined me. And it had happened many times before... Not this delightful doctor. He launched into a half-hearted explanation as he tried to justify why he couldn't examine me.

That's right, a doctor refused to examine me because I was in a wheelchair.

It had never been a problem before but he clearly struggled with the concept that, although I can just about walk, I wasn't able to mobilise onto the bed. I didn't have the energy to argue, so following his refusal we were sent back to the start to be triaged again.

This time I was seen by a different nurse and sent to another area to have bloods and a urine sample taken. I once again waited to be seen by a doctor, but this time they examined me while I was sat in my wheelchair. Testing confirmed it was an infection and again I was given antibiotics and sent home. Thankfully it was all over pretty quickly. Little did I know that I'd be back for a return visit to the hospital very soo n.

I had been taking the antibiotics as directed for a few days and had just been put to bed by my carer around 10pm on the Wednesday evening. I laid on my left hand side as I do every night and started scrolling through TikTok. I noticed a feeling of discomfort on my right hand side, near the bottom of my ribcage. I thought it might be a cramp or trapped wind and that it would soon resolve itself. The thing was, it didn't. By the time James came to bed around midnight, the discomfort had increased. Now it wasn't uncomfortable, it was painful. I tried moving into different positions to see if that gave any respite, but it didn't. It kept on hurting with every minute that passed.

I watched my bedside clock as the hours rolled by. I still believed it would subside and I was restless because I couldn't get comfortable. By now it was around 4am and I could see it starting to get light outside. I thought I could wait until morning but, by 6am, James woke up as he could tell something wasn't right. I was now breathless with pain. "Call 111," I said. They took a report and said someone would call within two hours. Nope, I was not waiting to be called, I knew I needed help – the pain had intensified so much that I was hunched over in pain. I needed to get to hospital, so James told Mum who was getting M ready. Thankfully, the hospital is only a short drive away, so we arrived around 7:30am to wait to see a nurse. I didn't have to wait long and, once I was seen, I was sent for blood to be taken, but the nurse couldn't find a vein. We were sent to wait in another area before a doctor called us in.

I consider that I have quite a high pain threshold and, while by now, I was in unbearable pain, I wasn't vocal about it. Mum had been stroking my hair and back as she could tell I was struggling as I rocked back and forth. I once again explained all that had gone on that week and I was taken aback when one nurse had the cheek to tell me, "You just need stronger painkillers and to give the antibiotics time to work". I do not condone physical acts of violence but if I had the ability to, I would have bopped the nurse on the nose at such a rude remark. I was angry at him saying this, despite having told him that my pain was at a ten and that this was a different pain to before. I imagine that, because when he physically examined me I wasn't screaming in pain, he could only assume it could not be that bad. I had to explain several times that, if I could, I would rip whatever this was out of my body. Thankfully, a senior doctor said he wanted to ultrasound the area. Within minutes he saw that my gall bladder looked fatty and so a CT scan was requested. During this time they must've tried at least ten times to get a line in for some fluids but failed at every opportunity as they put the needle in. Nothing came as close to the pain I was in.

I was sent to another department to wait. By this point, I'd had no pain relief whatsoever, and it was continuing to intensify. By the time I'd had the scan and gone back to wait, I knew that I needed pain relief. Mum asked, following which I was given some morphine. At last! It wasn't long after that my CT results came through which confirmed that my gall bladder was inflamed. I was told I would be admitted to the surgical ward. Once on the ward, they undertook their necessary observations and gave more pain relief – which finally had the pain under control. While I waited for a bed to become available, I got chatting to a lovely nurse, Hannah, who alleviated some of my anxiety and who took great care of me. I spoke openly about life with MND, and nothing was too much trouble for her. Within a few hours, I was moved onto a ward, which is where I would stay. As I couldn't use my call bell, they made sure that I was opposite the ward nurses' station, and my bed was directly opposite the long hallway which ran the entire length of the unit. It was the prime people-watching position!

I was soon visited by several consultants, who explained that they would need to treat the infection before being invited back to have my gall bladder removed. My main worry on the ward was that the staff wouldn't know how to care for a patient with MND. Thankfully the nightshift nurse and support workers knew exactly how to safely move me for bedtime. The only annoying thing was that I was woken every three hours for observations to be taken.

I was on a men's ward and was the youngest there. Some kept themselves to themselves, whereas I was quite happy to chat to staff and others on the ward to pass time. Karl, a fifty-something East Ender was in the bed to my right and it didn't take him long to see that I was dependent on others. He got Mum's attention one afternoon and said that he'd look after me, and he did exactly that for the rest of my stay. He brought me drinks from the hospital shop and came over to my bed with his laptop so we could watch films together. We chatted from our beds every day, putting the world to rights, and also having a moan to staff about several issues... more on that later. Karl and I swapped numbers and have kept in touch, and I thank him for the comfort and support he gave me and my family.

To my left was Len, who arrived the day after me and was suffering with severe nausea. I spoke to him the following morning to ask if he was feeling better. Thankfully his nausea had stopped but he needed an operation to sort a few things out. We spoke a lot and he, like Karl, took me under his wing. He went down for an operation a few days later and he was in my thoughts all day, until he came back up to the ward that evening. I also kept in touch with him and he really was a lovely man to me. Karl and Len were people that I wouldn't be likely speak to ordinarily, but their friendship and care was comforting. It was another reminder to not judge a book by its cover.

My love for people-watching made me realise two things throughout my stay. Our beloved NHS employs some amazing people, but also people who shouldn't be there. I was repeatedly shocked by the attitude, lack of compassion and care from certain staff. Some I wouldn't see for the majority of their shift. I also saw staff refusing to take instructions from senior staff. I had repeated issues with staff who claimed to have no idea how to move and reposition me safely, both in and out of bed. I was having to direct them as to how to do it. This was fed back to senior staff, who assured me that all staff knew how to do this. Sadly, it continued to happen and I very much felt like the problem. Further complaints were made, because I didn't want others in my position to suffer from the same experience.

Finally, there were staff there who went above and beyond like Hannah. On one shift, I immediately noticed Karen, a Clinical Support Worker who worked tirelessly from the start. Within her first hour on shift she had completed about 20 tasks. While she was based on another ward, she worked across the entire unit to make sure certain jobs got done. It was upon noticing me and my needs that she asked if I had been washed or out of bed – I hadn't. "Right, that's it, I'm getting you out of bed," she said. That's exactly what she did on each shift she was there and I felt so much better for it. Every shift, I watched how hard she worked from start to finish.

Throughout my stay I was pumped full of fluids along with antibiotics, and after six days I was discharged, as my infection markers had dramatically reduced. I was sent on my way with a concoction of medication to take and thankfully there have been no flare ups since. I'm currently waiting on a date for surgery, so hopefully, it won't be too long until my gall bladder is removed. The only downside is following a low fat diet, as I am losing weight which I cannot really afford to lose. This is because those living with MND are encouraged to have high fat diets. Nobody had to tell me twice to eat all the pies and cakes! It's quite possibly the only illness where you are told to go against medical advice to follow a healthy lifestyle. There is research to suggest that high fat provides the neurons with a thicker sheath coating them. So in turn, that may mean that the muscle wastage is slower. Naturally wasting muscles mean weight loss is inevitable, but it is difficult to put weight on once it is lost. Weight losses can be significant; this coupled with swallowing and choking concerns leads MND warriors to be fitted with a feeding tube such as a PEG – Percutaneous Endoscopic Gastrostomy. A small procedure normally carried out under sedation allows for a feeding tube to be inserted into the stomach through the abdominal wall. This means that liquids such as medications, fluids and nutrition can be administered directly into the stomach. So following a low fat diet is making me lose weight I really don't want to lose.

# Chapter 15: Parenting

Becoming a parent was not something that I had ever thought was possible in my lifetime, I never felt the pressure that this was something I had to do. Throughout my 20s, I didn't feel that it was going to happen and it wasn't until I met James that those feelings shifted into feeling that perhaps it was something I wanted to pursue.

One sunny Sunday afternoon, we visited Greenwich, and stopped for a drink at a pub along the river. We had been married for a few years by this point and the conversation soon turned to the future; we both said that we were interested to pursue adoption. No pressure was placed upon either of us to commit to it and we agreed that if it felt too much, we wouldn't pursue it any further. We wanted to know more before making any firm decisions. We contacted an adoption agency that we both liked, attending an evening information event before deciding to formally register with them. We soon proceeded with stage one, which was mainly lots of admin and some in-person training. Stage two soon followed; it involved lengthy meetings with our social worker to discuss all things parenting. At the same time, I had to gain experience of working with children I didn't know, so I spent a year volunteering at our local Beaver unit.

Once approved by an independent panel to adopt, it was then a case of looking at children's profiles to see if we thought any were suitable matches. It wasn't too long before we saw M's and we both thought we would be a good match for him. Following months of emails and visits, his social workers agreed and we were shortlisted. Another approval panel followed but, due to some last minute legal barriers, M didn't come home until months later. We were now parents to a beautiful toddler! We had to wait for several months before applying to the court for an Adoption Order. After various delays throughout this process, we eventually became his legal parents the following year.

Even though we had prepared for his arrival, it was still a shock to become parents overnight. I constantly felt as though we were winging it, something I now know is entirely normal. We learnt so much and there certainly were periods that I struggled with, missing life pre-parenthood and adjusting to life with a toddler. Before we knew it, he had started school and he soon settled in.

M first noticed my struggle with the lack of strength when I couldn't open a drink for him one lunchtime. He didn't say anything but he looked at me with confusion. As time went on and my strength weakened, I began asking him to open packages and drinks. He always did so and never once questioned it. It wasn't long before I had my first fall – I had fallen off a stool that I was sat on to read him a bedtime story. I managed to get myself up, and again he never questioned me about why it happened.

He has always loved being helpful, and so made himself useful whenever he was asked to help putting my footwear on. I do feel guilty, despite his helpful nature, because he is doing things that many children of his age would never have to do. However, I hope this will give him an understanding of being a young carer and will mean he'll grow up to be a rounded individual with a broad knowledge of the world.

"Daddy, will your arms get better?" He said this so innocently when he could see my arms were not able to mobilise without help. I very carefully had to tell him my arms would not get better, and that I was OK with that because there were many other things that I can do. I expected him to perhaps ask why, but he didn't and carried on without hesitation.

Three years on and, every now and then, he still asks about my arms, but doesn't question anything. He often kisses my arms which is his way of acknowledging they are poorly. I try to make things as fun as possible and he occasionally plays with my arms. We have chosen to not share too much about my illness, but give him information as and when we believe it is the right time.

The first time he saw me on my mobility scooter, his face was priceless. He asked why I needed it; once I explained it was there to support my tired legs, he said no more. I made it fun when I was out with him by turning the speed up and racing him home! It was the same with my power chair; also, including him in it has helped us to talk about mobility.

Last summer he came home from school one day and I could tell something wasn't right with him. I chatted to him and it transpired that something had been said by another child at school about me being in a wheelchair, which had upset him. I comforted him about this not bothering me and said that, just because I use a wheelchair, it doesn't stop me. I still achieve things, but I do them differently. We mentioned his emotional concerns to the school and they held an assembly a few days later about diversity and inclusion. What we have tried to do is to show M that in the face of adversity, anything is possible.

Last summer, we watched the Paris Olympics and Paralympics on television with keen interest. It gave us the opportunity to explain and show M that disability didn't stop athletes from achieving their dreams. It really helped him being able to see Paralympians doing remarkable things. Many children and adults do not see disability frequently enough, and wheelchair users are a minority, so I hope that, by being seen and showing others that we are just like them, it allows us to live harmoniously.

Parenting while living with MND has some challenges, but also has positive moments too. While I am not able to match the physical demands parenting requires, I am still able to parent him. A life-limiting illness does not mean being "incapable". The positives are that we really cherish the time and memories; it has forced me to be more present and available. With the good comes the bad, MND means it is likely I will not see him start secondary school or his teenage years and beyond. This is heartbreaking, but we make the most of what we have now.

Being diagnosed at 35, I have struggled to find others in my position. I have found it difficult to relate to others who are diagnosed at a different point in their lives. Having a young family means that, when my time comes, they will be living and growing with grief from a young age. As much as I try to remain and project a positive outlook, I'm angry for what it takes away from me.

As much as children are resilient, they can internalise emotions, as they may not know how to explain clearly or how to share. We encourage M as much as we can to chat through anything on his mind, but it's not always clear for us to see when he may need to offload. Interestingly enough, we see behaviours from time to time that go back to being a baby and toddler. This is quite common for children who seek comfort from these early years, and the parenting they either enjoyed or missed. For now, M knows very little about my illness but, at the same time, he isn't silly. He has seen me go from being able-bodied to having limited mobility and having carers visit every day. He will continue to see me deteriorate and we know he will want to know more. We have to juggle how much he needs to know as opposed to remaining and living as a child for as long as possible.

M, like most children, is naturally inquisitive and will ask questions about anything he sees. We have given him an age appropriate explanation of my symptoms, but presently he doesn't know all too much about what will continue to happen, but it does make me wonder the questions he may ask.

I am often asked if I am ever in pain and what having MND feels like. Firstly, the illness itself isn't painful. I do however encounter huge discomfort with cramps all over my body. I wouldn't describe these as normal cramps, they are far more intense than that. I was prescribed quinine sulphate to help alleviate the cramps. I was also advised drinking tonic water would help as it contains quinine, but I took a pass on that as it's a rancid liquid to drink. I'm sure a medicinal gin and tonic would help though – every cloud and all that.

The only way I can describe the illness is that I don't have the ability to mobilise my arms, so more or less have everything done for me. Got a hair in your eye? An annoying itch on your nose or want to shoo away an irritating fly? Need to blow your nose? You simply can't do any of it. So if you're on your own with nobody in earshot, you just have to put up with it, which can be deeply frustrating. My arms flail about but, other than shoulder shrugs, I have very limited movement.

MND has taught me many things; above all else it made me realise the things I took for granted that I no longer have the ability to do. It's another reminder that the illness continually takes from you. The only thing it will not take is who I am and what makes me, me. I learnt that all of us are never far from a life-limiting illness and that we should all strive to live the fullest life.

I miss...

- Hugging people
- Being able to run
- Having a bath
- Taking M for a day out by myself
- Holding a pen and being able to write
- Cooking a meal
- Taking Ralph for a walk

- Driving a car
- Making a coffee
- Walking upstairs/downstairs
- Swimming
- Chugging a drink to quench my thirst
- Dressing myself
- Spontaneous weekends away
- Mowing the lawn
- Dancing
- Holding a 99' ice cream
- Intimacy

# Chapter 16: Grief & Death

Grief is, or can be, a complex emotion to navigate. My first experiences of it came following the passing of people outside my family. The first funeral I went to, I was around 16 and I found the experience highly emotional but comforting, because hundreds had come to pay their respects. It was a huge outpouring of love for this person who had unexpectedly passed away. Over the next decade, all four of my grandparents died – the emotions hit differently each time. These were people who had helped raise me, and of whom I had many personal memories. My grief wasn't like it had been before; I found that it would bubble up throughout my life in unexpected moments. It may be a smell, a moment, place or memory that would make me grieve their losses years later.

What I've learnt is that grief is a profoundly personal emotion. People grieve in many different ways; there is no handbook for how to grieve. Some will pass judgement because they don't agree with how someone choses to, but it's not their grief to experience. My own grief would pop up from time to time, but it wasn't until I became a parent that I would encounter a newfound grief that was unlike anything I had felt before.

Becoming a parent to M in 2020 was equally rewarding and challenging. The UK adoption process is a lengthy process to navigate. It took several years to go through it before our son came home in 2020. At this point, we were still in the Coronavirus pandemic which brought its own challenges. However, as time passed, becoming parents changed our lives. We couldn't do things we had done before, like a day or evening out, we now had to think as a family. It was about a year or so later that I missed and pined for my pre-parenting life and was grieving for my old life. I spoke openly about post-adoption depression on my YouTube vlog "Daddy, Dad & Me", learning that it's absolutely fine to have that grief. Many others have shared with us their pre-parenting grief and thanked us for sharing that with them.

As time and as my condition progresses, my life and body have changed. I noticed last year that two years of life with MND meant I wasn't able to do much of what I had before. My body was and still is changing in many ways. Despite living in that body, looking at photos of me being able-bodied shows me just how much has changed. I miss the person I used to be and all the things I could do. I struggled with my identity as my life and social circle shrank, I was having to accept my new life as a wheelchair user. That grief will continue to evolve and is likely to manifest and present itself for the rest of my life. Grief ties in with my identity and I know that I am not the same person I was in 2 022.

We all die. The goal isn't to live forever, but to create something that will.

Being told you're going to die early is life-changing and shifts perspective instantly. I remember in the days following diagnosis that my worry was that I would die within months, without having put any plans in place for my final wishes. I felt out of control and I gravitated towards things that I could manage. Death is not something I had thought about; who does?! It wasn't until I was faced with my own mortality that I gave it some proper thought. It was a comment during a meeting with my neurologist that prompted me to take action; "Death is inevitable for us all, but very few plan for it".

Self-reflection made me realise that everybody I had known who died, didn't know they were going to – they hadn't made any plans for their final wishes. Funerals had been planned by families without knowing if they had any specific wishes. I didn't want my family to worry about whether I wanted songs by Rod Stewart or Right Said Fred to be played at my funeral. (The answer is neither in case you're wondering!) I had now been told my due date was going to be much earlier and so I needed to do something about it. By this, I mean that my life will end much sooner than I hoped, I have made it clear that I do not want to know how long is left; just let me live my life as worry-free as I can. There will be others who do want to know, so you have to do what is right for you.

At first I was apprehensive of speaking about my death, because it felt odd to want to speak openly about it. I soon realised that this is why the Brits don't talk about a subject that is considered taboo. It makes us feel uncomfortable and it isn't perceived as "normal". The only way to normalise and make others comfortable is to speak about it, and that's exactly what I've been doing ever since. There are religions and cultures that celebrate and honour death; if it's good enough for them, it's good enough for me.

Within a month of diagnosis, I had set up my own funeral plan; this gave me the comfort of knowing that the financial cost would be covered. The plan has now been paid, so that has given me the security of knowing that my family do not need to worry about finances at an already difficult time.

Once my plan was set up, I began to think about my death, and I still do. I wondered what it would be like and whether it would be a "good death". That may sound weird but death isn't always ugly – it can be peaceful and tranquil. The more I thought about my passing, the more I knew I had to start documenting my final wishes. So I set up a folder on my computer and over time I have added to it. I revisit it from time to time and update it if things have changed, or if I want to add to it. I have documented everything from who to notify, what I want to wear, songs I want played, my own eulogy and more. It feels important to me to plan for all of this because I want to know that it was done in the way I wanted.

I encourage you all to spend some time noting down your wishes and letting someone know, or sharing it with them. Not a single one of us knows what will happen to us at any time. Life is unpredictable, and growing old is not a privilege that we will all get to enjoy. MND has taught me so much but, most importantly, it has shown me we should live in the moment and be present. Smile at others. Be the reason to make others smile. Do not take for granted the idea that tomorrow is guaranteed.

# Chapter 17: Therapy

I firmly believe that we could all benefit from therapy. We have all experienced difficulties and challenges in life, one way or another. Having the ability to offload your mind to someone who has no emotional connection to you is something I strongly recommend.

I became a Mental Health First Aider in 2021, as I have always thought I am quite attuned to not only my own mental health but that of others too. The training enabled the group of us to share our own lived experience of mental health, as well as understanding what had led us to the training. I have had relatively good mental health for most of my life, but have had moments when it suffered. I had worked through these in time and reminded myself to be kind. So it came as somewhat of a surprise when my mental health declined in 2024. I clearly wasn't taking my own medicine or advice.

When I was diagnosed in 2022 with a terminal illness, my mental health weirdly didn't suffer straight away, as some may think. If anything, I had a fantastic outlook, because so much was going on and I was speaking to many people on a daily basis. That meant I could offload any worries. As I said, my symptoms were invisible to the outside world for the first year and, although my body was slowly changing, I found it easy to adapt. It was as time and my illness progressed and relationships changed that I noticed a decline in my overall outlook on life. I kept this hidden for a while, as the burden of guilt grew within me, as I watched the pressure and pain of those around me struggle in their own way.

As my disability advanced and I slowly lost independence, I tried to continue living as normally as I could but, with so much going on, I couldn't keep all the plates spinning. I tried not to think about what my illness would look like in the future but, every now and then, my mind would wander – knowing things will only get worse weighed heavy on me. I also struggled looking at photographs of myself and pined to have my old body back. I was envious of my own body and realised I had taken it for granted, along with all the amazing things it does without me ever thinking about them. It was only as I began to struggle doing the simple things that I wrestled with my thoughts. I believed it would be easier if I wasn't here. I never acted on those thoughts, but I certainly thought of ways to end my existence.

It was at this time that I realised something had to give – I took time away from work so I could receive the support I needed. Having not taken any time off since diagnosis had clearly taken its toll on me emotionally, physically and mentally. Without realising it, I had suppressed a lot and, while I chose to keep working full-time, it had masked many things. I had always thought the time that had passed since diagnosis had been a long time, but it was only when seeking help that somebody made me realise in comparison to the rest of my life, three years was nothing. In those three years, everything in my life had changed; how on earth could this *not* affect me? I had to learn that now, I needed to be kind to myself and get the help I needed.

I went on to receive cognitive behavioural therapy (CBT), which I was told is a common therapy for those living with chronic and life-limiting illnesses. This type of therapy is there to help in identifying and changing negative thought patterns. It isn't for everyone, and it's about finding what works for you. I found the therapy beneficial and it helped me speak about my negative thoughts and work through each of these to understand why I felt a particular way. It really helped me to not apportion any blame and guilt to the life I was now living. I had previously absorbed so much of everything around me that it weighed heavy on me, let alone while living life every day. I needed to let that go and focus on shifting my mindset. This will be a constant work in progress, and therapy will be something I will probably revisit again.

I have also struggled with my identity, because MND has meant I am not able to live exactly as I did before. I cannot go anywhere without someone knowing where I am. Chuck in a wheelchair to daily life and it has blurred my identity even more. I lost sight of who I was and I felt useless. I felt that I was merely existing and ultimately waiting until the inevitable happened. I have had to accept all of these new additions to my life, without question. Therapy helped me to realise that these physical things do not make my identity. While many parts of my life have changed, they don't make me the person that I am.

Therapy made me realise that a life-changing illness doesn't mean I stop being me. It has shown me that there is so much life that is yet to be lived. I encourage everyone reading this to consider therapy. It gave me the opportunity to let someone in – someone who didn't know me or my situation, but could help work through negative thoughts and give me the tools I need to approach these things in the times ahead.

# Chapter 18: How to Feel when Your Husband is Dying

James Hayden-Harler

There's no guidebook on how to navigate a terminal diagnosis; there are no rules. My chapter could be titled "learning to live while the person you love slowly dies", because that describes exactly what is happening.

When Sam was diagnosed with MND, the bottom completely dropped out of our world. The list of questions that we had was endless, and there were some that we could not get answers to.

There were medical questions such as:

- How does the disease progress?
- What is the life expectancy?
- Will it hurt? Will he suffer?

Then there are the practical and emotional questions:

- What do we need to do about living arrangements?
- What financial support can we get?
- Will I be able to continue to work or look after our son?

- How will I cope watching Sam deteriorate?

Your brain just goes into overdrive; you have to try not to think about all these questions at the same time or you drive yourself mad.

One of my biggest worries, which still exists, is how our will son cope with this. Will he grow up not remembering his dad? How will he remember Sam when he's older? Will he only remember him being ill? What will happen to him if something happens to me? What will happen when Sam goes? How am I expected to look after M as well as myself? I can't leave it all to my in-laws – they have their own grieving process.

I am anxious that I won't even be able to function myself and process what is happening, so how can I expect a child to do that without any help? These are thoughts I have daily, but that I have to try and ignore – as I can't control this now.

A lot of people compare MND with cancer, as that is most people's frame of reference for a terminal diagnosis. But with cancer there is often a hope that treatment or operations could work. With MND there is no hope. There is no proof of a drug that extends life. With cancer, people can often be given a timeline and an order in which changes may occur... with MND you can't. It affects everyone differently and at different speeds. There is no timeline. You have no hope.

The day Sam got his diagnosis is the day I started grieving.

Some people find that hard to grasp, but, when there is a terminal diagnosis, you do not just grieve the person. I began grieving for the life that we would never have, the time we would never spend together and everything our son would miss growing up; I am grieving for the fact that, when I look back in years to come, the happy memories will be tarred with a sadness that overtakes them.

I've learnt that grief comes, not only in waves, but in cycles. For every element of your life and the person that you grieve, there is a separate cycle. At any one time it is thought that you can be processing seven cycles of grief, at different stages. For the loved ones of someone with a diagnosis of MND, it's a constant cycle of grief that keeps going. Every time something changes. it starts a new cycle, and it's exhausting. Grief is exhausting!

Sometimes I am consumed by sadness and just cry all the time; just the smallest thing can set me off. Sometimes I am consumed by anger and just want to throw things and shout at people. Emotions are a complicated thing and, when your life is turned upside down and so much changes, your emotions are very close to the surface.

I often feel very lonely. I don't have any close family that I am in contact with (that's all another story). My mother died in 2013. She was my closest person; we used to speak daily and I would tell her everything, and she was my sounding board. I have missed her so much over the last 12 years, and especially the last three, since Sam's diagnosis. Of course I have friends, but of those, only one lives close to us, the rest live a good three and a half hour drive away. It's amazing that, when you do a job where you work with over 100 people and live in a house with five other people, you can feel so alone, isolated and, often, misunderstood.

As well as sadness and loneliness, there are the feelings of guilt. Feeling guilty that it's happening to Sam and not me. Feeling guilty for my behaviour, lashing out and being frustrated. Feeling guilty that

I am spreading myself too thin, or working too much. Feeling guilty for taking time for myself. (As I've learnt, self-care is important, but when you know there are things that need your attention, the guilt creeps in.) My overriding emotion is often guilt.

One of the things I have struggled with most is the lack of control. Anyone that knows me will know that I like to plan and, in most situations, I know what is going to happen. You can't control MND, *it* has the control. It has controlled where we live, who we live with, when we can go out, where we can go out and sometimes who with.

Stupid things like trying to get all of us out of the house now takes longer, and it keeps changing as Sam's mobility declines. We have to constantly adapt, and that doesn't happen overnight. You have to find new ways of doing things, like getting dressed or undressed. We've had to learn how to use hoists, slide sheets and fall chairs. We've had bed lifts installed (and uninstalled... as it was noisy), an alarm system for when Sam needs something, a wash and dry toilet and a full body air dryer. As Sam declines, we will need to have more pieces of equipment and learn how to use them.

Do relationships change? Yes of course they do, I think it's only natural when one person becomes more of a care giver. Marriage vows are in sickness and in health, and I think it's fair to say that when you take them most people assume you won't need to become a care giver until later in life. I never thought that I would have to be washing and dressing my husband after just six years of marriage. Of course I did it, because I love Sam. But there was a point when it became too much and I was beginning to hurt myself and get back ache. There's no training for how to look after someone. You don't have lessons in how to wash or dress another person. You just have to make it up as you go along. And to be honest, I think we did a pretty good job. We are lucky that we have now have access to carers to come in each day and wash and dress Sam.

But it's not just my relationship with Sam; my relationship with our son has become closer, as I am aware at some point I will be a single parent. My relationship with my in-laws has changed; we now live together, and that brings challenges for us all – but ultimately it's the situation that works best for us in the long run. All of us have had to make sacrifices and have had our lives uprooted.

Am I coping? Just about. I would best describe it as "surviving". Day by day, hour by hour, minute by minute. People who see social media posts, or people you talk to about what's happening, often say I'm a "superstar", "brave" or a "shining example". But what they don't see is the anger I feel, how I slam doors or shout and scream when something minor doesn't go my way. They don't see how the *tiniest* thing can send me over the edge.

I'm not proud of everything I have done on this journey so far, I've made some big mistakes that have affected our relationship. When people say "I don't know how you do it", the truth is some days I can't. There are days when everything gets on top of me and I just can't face having to be a strong and positive individual. Humans can put on a brave face, and I did it for years. But in January 2025 I reached a point where I couldn't do it any longer and I decided I was going to take my own life. I now understand that, at that point, I had (at least what we used to call) a complete breakdown, mentally and physically. As well as the breakdown, I had complete burn-out. I reached a point where

I felt I had no positivity left in me and had compassion fatigue. I was unable be empathetic and was struggling to engage with people on the level I needed to. I was emotionally exhausted and had no energy for anything. Things that normally brought me joy were no longer doing that, and it felt like I was stuck in a hamster wheel. I'd get annoyed at the smallest thing. This not only affected my relationships within the house, but with friends and at work also. I began to worry that I was not able to do my job and I was starting to get a reputation for not coping well. I didn't know how to channel the little energy I have left. Did I use it for our son, for Sam, for myself or for work? Which things did I let go and fall by the wayside? And it was me and my personal care that fell by the wayside.

Through rest, therapy and support, I am improving, but there are days when things can still get really dark. It often feels like I am not allowed to feel these emotions, that I am expected to somehow block them out and be strong all the time. That's what I did and how I ended up in the situation I was in.

I'm now not afraid to show my emotions or say that I'm struggling. When you are in a position where you are looking after so many people in a job, and some of those people have very real problems, you bury your emotions and show up for them. To listen, to advise, and to help. Burying emotions takes energy, and putting on the brave face takes energy. High-functioning depression is exhausting.

Now it's not all doom, gloom and me being depressed; since Sam's diagnosis we have probably lived a more full life. Sam and I have been back to New York (and stayed at the Plaza), we've been on a Disney Cruise around the Caribbean and been to Mexico. We've seen multiple shows, concerts and comedians. We've been to fireworks every year, done Christmas films with live orchestras, been to panto and wandered the Christmas lights. We did get to a point in the first year post-diagnosis where we were trying to cram too much in. Living life to the full is exhausting.

There are times when you have to laugh, and we do laugh at the disease. When walking Sam around the house I walk backwards holding his arms up – I say it's "Thriller time". Or I say "one, two, three... one, two, three..." – like we are dancing some kind of waltz. Sam will make jokes about not being able to do things too.

Sam living with this disease has really opened our eyes to living as a disabled person and how you get treated. Whenever Sam is in his wheelchair, we get stared at – I now stare people out. We've also had situations where, just because Sam is in the chair people ignore him and only talk to me, or they will talk to him like he can't understand what they are saying.

Disabled access is still an issue that needs to be looked at in this country. Many venues say they are accessible and have level access, when in fact they don't. Multiple times we have gone somewhere and there is a lip, or a small step to gain access – this is *not* level access. Until you have been in a wheelchair, or accompanied someone in one, I don't think you realise just how inaccessible the world can be.

We try to go to see as much theatre, comedy, concerts etc. as we can, but it can be extremely difficult if we want it to be more than just Sam and me. For example, most venues (theatre, concert halls and arenas) only allow space for a wheelchair and one companion, so if we want to see something as a family of three, or attend a concert with friends, we are not able to sit together as there are no allowances for this. Working in theatre, I understand that it's not always possible, but it doesn't make it any less frustrating. Not being able to sit together is not an enjoyable experience and does nothing to help the person in the wheelchair feel included or treated like everyone else.

One of my biggest gripes with accessibility is *how* in 2025 is it not possible to take your wheelchair on an aeroplane? Why does anyone who is disabled have to be subjected to being put into the tiniest of transfer chairs, strapped in and wheeled down the aisle for all to stare at? There is no dignity in this. And unless you can transfer yourself, you are not able to get on the plane. Airlines should be forced to be more accessible, in my opinion.

There has been so much loss already, and there will continue to be. I don't just mean the loss of Sam or his body failing him. As a family, we have a loss of choice and a loss of freedom. Every day I wake up and this terrible, robbing disease is the first thing I think about. This disease steals my joy. It makes me feel unhappy and it makes me cry, sometimes for no apparent reason. It makes me feel lonely.

Eventually this disease will steal my husband. But the husband I know, the husband I married will be gone long before then. I will always love him, even after he is gone and nobody will ever be able to replace him and share the experiences we have been through together.

So how would I describe my journey with MND so far? Powerful, hard, isolating, lonely, frustrating, angry, depressing, hurtful, full of grief and exhausting.

# Chapter 19: The Bucket List

Prior to my MND diagnosis I never really took stock of the things I have accomplished in life, I was too busy making memories and having fun. That soon changed and I took time noting all the things I had accomplished and made a list of things I wanted to tick off. "Sam & The Bucket List" was launched in 2022, several weeks post-diagnosis!

It's saved on my blog where you'll find an up-to-date progress chart for how much I am yet to complete. The list is accurate as of July 2025. As I said, I poke fun at my illness (it's a great coping mechanism) and so it only felt right to title the blog "When Life Hands You Lemons".

1. **Make Fresh Lemonade, of course!**

   Along with our son, under, my close supervision, we made fresh lemonade on my 38th birthday in 2024.

2. **Fall in love**

   I met my husband in 2013 and the rest, as they say, is history.

3. **Get engaged**

   We got engaged on 25 July 2015 in the grounds of the secret garden at the Ashdown Park Country Club Hotel.

4. **Get Married**

We tied in the knot at Buxted Park Hotel on 24 July 2016.

5. **Have a family**

   Our family became complete when Little Man came home in the Summer of 2020.

6. **Own a dog**

   Ralph, our beloved and very cheeky Dachshund arrived in April 2017 at five months old and we've been sausage mad ever since!

7. **Go on safari**

   As part of our honeymoon, we spent four days on safari in the Masai Mara, Kenya. It was a once-in-a-lifetime experience seeing wild animals in their natural habitat. We were lucky to witness a baby giraffe that had just been born. A truly magical memory.

8. **Ride a hot air balloon**

   On day three of our honeymoon we caught a very early morning ride to take a ride in a hot air balloon. Nothing can beat watching the sun rise over the Masai Mara whilst you are a few thousand feet in the air watching the world below come to life.

9. **See the Northern Lights**

   We spent several days in Iceland and, one night, we were very lucky enough to see them.

10. **Run a marathon**

I ran the London Marathon in 2014 and 2015 for the Juvenile Diabetes Research Foundation (JDRF) and Children with Cancer UK. I also walked the Shine Night Walk in 2019.

11. **Watch my friends get married**

    I have watched my beautiful friends marry and felt lucky to have shared their special days.

12. **Forgive someone**

    I won't say too much about this, but having forgiven someone has given me strength to accept differences and to move on with what really matters. You realise who and what matters when you need them.

13. **Donate blood as a gay man**

    January 2021 saw me being able to donate, finally after many years of gay men not being able to. Soon after donating I received an update to advise that my blood had been used for someone in need. I'm no longer able to donate but encourage anyone that is able to sign up. Free drink and biscuits too!

14. **Experience live theatre**

    My love of theatre has enabled me to see so much over the years, and for that I am very thankful. I still aim to watch as much theatre as I can. MND won't stop me.

15. **Visit New York**

    I first visited NYC in 2014 with my sister and then again in 2019 and 2022 – it's a city that I could not help falling in love with.

16. **Appear on TV to raise awareness of MND**

    Thanks to ITV; they arranged for me to appear on *Good Morning Britain* speaking about my own experience of living with MND.

17. **Go to an Adele concert**

    I have seen my idol Adele several times and, in 2023, I got to see her again in Hyde Park.

18. **Learn to drive**

    2006 saw me passing my driving test, first time, with only one minor.

19. **Watch the sunset in Guernsey**

    I've spent many times in Guernsey on family holidays and have an abundance of memories. I got to go back one final time in summer 2024 to say goodbye. I will have some of my ashes scattered there.

20. **Fly first class**

21. **Raise £50,000 for the MND Association**

    I will do everything possible to raise as much as I can in the fight against MND. As of 2025 I have raised circa £20,000.

22. **Afternoon tea at The Ritz**

    We enjoyed a festive afternoon tea on New Year's Day 2023. We were entertained by a quartet singing Christmas classics and M was given his very own Ritz bear.

23. **Write a book**

    Thanks to the publication of this book, I am now a published author!

24. **Throw a party for my family and friends**

    I am hoping to throw a bash for my 40th in August. If I'm not here, I still want it to happen.

25. **Bingo**

    I must have been an old lady in a previous life, but I've never been to a bingo hall to play. Watch this space.

26. **Meet/speak with Adele**

    You may have guessed that I'm an Adele fan. I wasn't able to see her perform during her Las Vegas residency but purchased the vinyl from her live shows. I'm hoping that the six degrees of separation means that someone can make this happen?!

27. **Create my own cologne**

28. **Holiday on a cruise**

    In April 2023, we embarked on a family cruise onboard the Disney cruise liner. We had a fantastic time visiting the Caribbean.

29. **To have made an impact on others**

    I consider this complete in that all the projects I have completed in the last three years have had a positive impact on others.

30. **Take time to appreciate nature**

    It's something very simple but I have found in my darkest days that nature has been deeply healing; it gives me a sense of freedom and peace. Definitely never under appreciate the power of Mother Nature.

31. **Go skinny dipping**

32. **Learn how to play an instrument**

33. **Attend a concert as a VIP and meet 'n' greet the artist**

34. **Tell at least one person a day that I love them**

    I have been very open with my feelings and always tell those around me that I love them. I want them to know that while I am still here, not when I am gone!

35. **Complete a random act of kindness with a stranger**

    In August 2023, I set up my own bucket list book club. The sole intention of the book club was to send books to people who were kindly able to place books in a place of their choosing. Once the books had been discovered, a small message from me had been left in the book, to share a little joy to the person and a little about my own journey, and to keep raising awareness of MND. You can join the book club on Facebook "Sam & The Bucket List Book Club".

36. **Meet a member of the Royal Family**

37. **Go to Cadbury World**

In February 2025 I visited and had a great time, plus so many chocolates were given throughout the tour.

38. **Visit Blackpool**

We visited during the summer of 2024 and it was a beautiful sunny day. The tower was great to go up and we made a weekend of it by staying in Nantwich, paying a visit to Emma Bridgewater.

39. **Let go of the past**

As they say, we live and learn. My diagnosis has shown me it's best not to hold onto the past, but to look ahead, and that continues to be my focus. What once bothered me, no longer does. Perspective is a wonderful thing.

40. **Plant a tree**

With eternal thanks to my friend Claire for arranging it, Scotney Castle agreed for a tree to be planted in my name, so it can grow and be visited in the years and decades ahead. If you're ever there, ask to see the tree planted by the Queen Mother; directly to its left is "my tree"!

41. **Stay At The Plaza Hotel, New York**

We visited NYC from the 1st to the 6th December 2022, and we stayed here; I totally lived my *Home Alone* dreams!

42. **Be an extra in a TV show or movie**

Thanks to people in the know, I spent some time on the set of Casualty as a supporting artist for a few days. You will see me in the opening scenes of series 37, episode 5!

43. **Ride on a sleeper train**

    This was so much fun to do on the Caledonian Sleeper Train; we had a beautiful weekend in Edinburgh. The train left London shortly before midnight and arrived in Glasgow around 7am.

44. **Set a world record**

45. **Go to the ballet at Christmas**

    James and I went to the Royal Opera House one Christmas Eve to watch "The Nutcracker". We had a great time and the atmosphere of the ballet was unforgettable.

46. **Ask those who know me what their favourite memories of our time together are**

    I asked my family and friends to share some of their memories of our time and, while most of them appears to relate to my younger "drinking days", it was a lovely wander down memory lane.

47. **Get to know our neighbours**

    We consider that we're very lucky to know our neighbours well.

48. **Have a family photoshoot**

    We've very kindly been gifted three photography sessions.

49. **Fly a kite!**

    We spent a week in Devon and I got to fly my kite up on Dartmoor. I loved it, what an experience!

50. **Make a photo book of my life**

51. **Plan my own funeral**

    I have planned it all and this has given me great comfort in knowing that my wishes will be followed.

52. **Ride in a limo**

53. **Play a prank on someone**

54. **Launch a naked charity photo calendar**

55. **Get my upper ear pierced**

    I had wanted to get this done for years, and finally did in 2022!

56. **Have a bonfire at night with toasted marshmallows**

    We were kindly sent a s'mores kit and they were delicious.

57. **Have a song request played on radio**

    Thanks to the lovely team at *Coronation Street*, they heard about my bucket list and were able to arrange with Zoe Ball's BBC Radio 2 breakfast show for me to have three songs played, live on an air! Zoe was super nice and shared with everybody details of my fundraising and passion for raising awareness. The songs were 'Who Do You Think You Are?' by The Spice Girls, "Crazy Horses" by The Osmonds and "1, 2, 3" by Gloria Estefan.

58. **Watch a film with a live orchestra**

    Claire booked us in to see *Titanic* at the Royal Albert Hall, with a live orchestra playing, and we loved it.

59. **Go to an open air concert**

We got to see *Six The Musical* performed at Hampton Court Palace. I've also seen Pink, Adele and Shania Twain in the open air.

60. **Leave a message in a random place for a stranger to find**

Thanks to those who took part in my bucket list book club, there are roughly 70 books spread across the globe, just waiting to be discovered!

61. **Give an heirloom to somebody I love**

One of the Christmas presents gifted to somebody in 2023 is an heirloom to be passed down throughout the generations.

62. **Watch the sunrise in a beautiful place**

We have been lucky to have travelled extensively, to countries including Antigua, Zanzibar, Kenya, St. Lucia, Dominican Republic, New York and Mauritius.

63. **Have my 15 minutes of fame**

What with my appearance on *Good Morning Britain* and multiple articles in The Mirror, The Sun and Daily Mail, in which I have been able to share my story, I have had my 15 minutes of fame.

64. **Pay for a stranger's drink**

I had the pleasure of buying drinks for a stranger and got chatting to them, and found out they too have experience of

MND.

65. **Get a tattoo**

    I have three – stars down my wrist, a tribal design on my back and an avocado on my other wrist.

66. **Write to 5 people who have inspired me**

67. **Donate to an animal shelter**

68. **Be in a TV show audience**

69. **Wish upon a star**

    I'm able to wish on my very own star, as we were kindly gifted stars named for us.

70. **Complete a 365-day photo project**

    Check out my photo project on my Instagram @samandthe-bucketlist

71. **Eat fish and chips on a seaside pier**

    Along with M, my sister and cousin, we went for a day out to Hastings, and so I got to enjoy my fish and chips. A memory savoured.

72. **Go to a night at the Proms at The Royal Albert Hall**

    James & I saw Cynthia Erivo at the Proms and she didn't disappoint. What an experience!

73. **Watch a Christmas Panto**

    For the last few years we have seen the panto in Crawley,

which was a great laugh and memory.

74. **Get driven around Brands Hatch or Silverstone**

    Huge thanks to the MND Association for organising a track day; I got the chance to be a passenger in a racing car at Brands Hatch!

75. **Try a battered Mars bar**

    I enjoyed this while in Edinburgh, what a delicious treat.

76. **Visit John O' Groats and Lands End**

    We had lots of family holidays when I was a child and I was lucky enough to visit both ends of the UK!

77. **Go to a silent disco**

78. **Watch a theatre show every day for a week**

    I had a very busy week in June 2022 and saw eight shows in a week; I loved it! The shows included "Book of Mormon", "Six", "Moulin Rouge", "My Fair Lady", "Dear Evan Hansen", "Legally Blonde" and "Back To The Future".

79. **Meet a Spice Girl**

80. **Pick a fun thing from my childhood to do with Little Man**

81. **Eat homemade burgers (you know who you are!)**

    On 19th March 2022 I got to enjoy my lovely burgers, made by my friend Jane. Loved them many moons ago and love them still.

82. **Have breakfast in bed**

83. **Make a bucket list**

    Done!

84. **Recreate a childhood photo**

85. **Visit my childhood homes**

    I took a walk down memory lane one afternoon with Little Man, showing him where I grew up. A nice memory to keep hold of.

86. **Go to the circus**

    We visited Giffords Circus and had a great time.

87. **Have a self-portrait**

    In Summer 2023, I had a self-portrait captured by the superbly talented Estelle.

88. **Climb the O2**

    Along with my chums, we climbed The O2 and had a great time. Although in true style I fell over after coming off and hit my head, cutting my head open! A trip to A&E and 4 stitches later, I was good to go.

89. **Go to a theme park for the day**

    We took Little Man to Legoland for the weekend and we had a fantastic time away.

90. **Create a blog**

    I'm very proud of the blog that I created to document our

adoption journey, life with Little Man and living with MND.

91. **Feed the ducks with Little Man**

We spent a lovely day in March 2022 at Leeds Castle with my friend and her beautiful boys. Little Man loved feeding the ducks!

92. **Write a poem inspired by my life**

**My poem 'Memories':**

*The old times are beautiful*
*more than those that are new*
*because they recall sweet memories*
*of all the things we used to do.*
*The buzz of my morning coffee,*□
*in my cherished "Daddy" mug,*□
*will be moments I'll savour forever,*□
*just like the comfort of a hug.*
*Photographs in albums,*□
*Letters written from the heart,*□
*Replay those old memories,*□
*from those we can't bear to part.*
*Listening to children playing,*□
*as they scream and cheer with delight,*□
*will one day be distant memories*
*that will then be out of sight.*
*As we watch the sun slowly set,*□
*As it fades from day to night,*□
*A party on a Caribbean beach*

*Under a moonlit starry night.*
*From the first hello, to our last goodbye,*□
*they become more precious every day,*□
*As all of these precious moments we shared,*□
*are the memories of yesterday.*

93. **Go fruit picking**

94. **A Christmas movie marathon**

December 2023. I headed over to my cousins to have our Christmas movie marathon, along with festive music, food and drink.

95. **Adopt an animal**

I receive some lovely post, and it was a surprise when I saw that I had very kindly been gifted the adoption of a WWF Panda by somebody.

96. **Write a letter to somebody I haven't spoken to in five or ten years**

Since the news of my diagnosis in March 2022, I have spoken to people with whom I had lost contact for various reasons, and can happily say that the past is well and truly behind us, as we look forward and to keep speaking to one another. It is never too late for forgiveness.

97. **Change my hair colour**

I'd always wanted to dye my hair but never had the confidence. 19th December 2022 changed all that – I went platinum!

98. **Leave an unexpected tip for someone**

    While in Edinburgh I was blown away by the service of a waitress and so I chose to give her an unexpected tip.

99. **Help someone tick something off their bucket list**

    James always wanted to dye his hair, so we **both** went platinum.

100. **Finally... complete my bucket list!**

# Chapter 20: So, What's Next?

My outlook over the last three years has not deviated; my aim is to continue living each day at a time. I firmly believe a positive outlook has given me the strength and energy to keep going. There will be not so great days that come along and I've learnt to accept these, knowing it will soon pass.

I really didn't expect to be working three years on, but having that routine and normality gives me the drive and focus to keep going. I will carry on working for as long as I possibly can, until my body says it's time. Thankfully I have the tools and technology in place that can allow this to happen.

I am approaching halfway on my fundraising mission and so I will be looking at ways to raise more for the MND Association, as well as continuing to raise awareness of MND however I can. Navigating from able-bodied to disabled hasn't stopped me; if anything it has made me more persistent.

There are many uncertainties with MND and other life-limiting illnesses which can manifest in feelings of being out of control. Rather than that, I turn my focus to what I *can* do and control. As I've said, I get asked from time to time if I want to be informed of how long I am for this world. Quite simply, no! I don't want to live for the rest of my days on a countdown; instead I try and cherish every day and not take things for granted. Remember; not a single one of us should take it that tomorrow is promised, because the reality is that anything can happen to any one of us, at any time. There are many life-limiting illnesses, and life has a way of reminding us just how fragile it is.

There are still things on my bucket list that I am yet to achieve and so that gives me the focus to tick them off. I have had lots of fun working my way through the list as well as seeing the generosity and love shown to me and my family.

MND presents many challenges which we have navigated and none of us know what is yet to come. I try not to envisage what the days ahead will look like; things can and are likely to change unexpectedly, and so I try not to focus on that as it does not serve me well. I will continue to live life with a positive mindset and a smile on my face. I know life will continue to throw more curveballs my way as things progress, but I refuse to let it control me.

Finally, enjoy the simple things. I try to find a pocket of happiness in every day. Whether that be the sun on my skin, a good catch up with a friend, a cup of coffee or lip-syncing to Adele. Find things that fill your cup and take time for some self-care.

Thanks again for reading my book and making a little boy's dream come true!

# Letters

MND DOESN'T JUST AFFECT me; it also hits and impacts many others. This isn't just my story to tell and I felt that it was important to share the many different experiences with you. I asked my family and friends to write to me, and so here they are.

## Hannah

Sam and I met when Sam joined the Direct Line Group Risk department in 2012. Sam and I were on different teams; however, it wasn't too long before we got to know each other. I have lovely memories of going for drinks after work in the local Wetherspoons and we'd chat so naturally like we'd known each other forever. I remember the open and honest chats we had during the early days of Sam's relationship with James and how smitten he was so early on! They were destined to be together, and James saw what we all saw – a gorgeous, lovely and kind soul with an outrageous sense of humour!!

It then got to the point where Sam had come to realise his existing role was no longer serving him, which coincided with a job vacancy coming up on my team (yay for me)! Therefore, in February 2014, following a successful interview, Sam became an Anti-Money Laundering Investigator and changed my team forever.

Sam was a superb member of my team. Enthusiastic, driven, energetic and determined. Sam brought such a magical energy to his work and always strived to do the right thing and make the world a better place. Sam would always volunteer to help me or his fellow teammates and would always be the one putting forward new ideas and innovative suggestions to make team processes more effective, in addition to raising awareness of our team's work across the other business areas. I loved working with Sam, which is why I couldn't believe it when I returned from maternity leave in July 2015 and Sam had flown the nest and moved onto his next career adventure! Sam had grown so much (professionally and personally) during his time on my team, and I felt so proud seeing him flourish and spread his wings, embracing new exciting opportunities ahead. Even though I was sad not to be working with Sam anymore, I knew deep down this wasn't the end of our friendship, this was just the beginning.

We continued to stay in touch with each other; at times we could go months without any contact but then could just pick straight up where we left off. Speaking to Sam has always felt so easy.

Following Sam and James becoming parents in 2020, we provided much needed support to one another navigating parenthood. With us both being parents of lively, feisty and energetic boys, sharing the blood, sweat and tears of parenting has been such valuable therapy which I am very grateful for (and long shall this continue!).

I have so many wonderful memories of time with Sam, and it has been so lovely to revisit them while writing my little slice of Sam's book. So that I don't take up too many pages (I could go on and on...!) I thought I'd better limit it to five standout memories:

1. Sam's obsession with Christmas. To date, I have not met anyone who loves Christmas more than Sam! For a number of years Sam hosted a Christmas gathering for close friends and family and he would go all out with festive decorations, food and drink – it was always a fabulous evening to remember and kicked off Christmas for me. This brings me nicely on to number 2...

2. Sam's favourite festive delicacy – the Brussels sprout sandwich. A very interesting concept but one I never felt brave enough to try! Sam would rave about these in the office and put forward a very compelling case!

3. Sam's frustration when forced to unnecessarily queue. Cue a stern tweet to the shop responsible in Bromley high street! Sam would never be rude, just quietly assertive. I always admired Sam's assertiveness in situations like this.

4. London Marathon (2014). What an inspiration! I loved hearing regular updates as Sam progressed through his marathon training plan. This was during the time Sam was on my team, so we'd often have a good natter about the ups and downs (chafed nipples spring to mind!) of marathon training. I remember hosting a cake sale at work with Sam to help raise money – this was a wonderful fundraising event and one of many that Sam organised to exceed his fundraising target. We were all so proud of Sam for such a tremendous achievement!

5. Sam and James' Wedding (2016) – the most beautiful day, full of style, class and love. Every minute of the day had been carefully thought out and I felt so honoured to be there with my husband Jim and many friends to witness our gorgeous Sam marry his soulmate.

I received the message on 5 March 2022. I remember it like it was yesterday, I was on my way to Alexandra Palace with Jim, my niece Gemma and her husband Harry. We were seeing the dance duo Disclosure, which we were all very excited about, especially me and Jim, as it was a very rare night out without the kids! The message came through and just from reading the first sentence, I could tell from the tone, it was not the usual happy, positive message from Sam. Something was wrong, and this was not good news.

I quietly scanned the message as we parked up and walked to the venue. I had heard of MND before, but at that point, I knew very little about it. I didn't know enough to be able to respond straight away; however I could not stop thinking about Sam all night and I felt so grateful to be out with loved ones and dancing, as if I was carefree.

When I got home, I got into bed and googled MND. My heart broke and the tears started rolling – I was now ready to respond. At 1.28am I responded "Thank you so much for sharing Sam, I can only imagine how difficult it must have been, to write all of this down and then share. I am here. For you, for James, for M – for all of you, in whatever capacity you need me. I will always be right here. I'll be ready, just give me a wink. Love you Sam xxxxx"

Empathy is my superpower, so hearing this news about someone I care so deeply about was very difficult to process. I couldn't even begin to imagine what Sam, James and their families were going through right now. I felt so helpless.

Since the diagnosis, our relationship has not only flourished, but it has also evolved. In 2022 I finally began my journey into Reiki healing. Now, I have wanted to train and qualify for years but due to one thing or another, the universe decided it hadn't been the right time until May 2022. As I worked my way up to my Level 3 Master Reiki degree, I saw Sam a number of times for Reiki healing sessions and am very grateful to Sam for being my guinea pig as I experimented with various music, tuning forks, pendulums and short guided meditations during our sessions.

It has been a really wonderful experience for me, connecting with Sam on a spiritual level and being able to create time and space for Sam to completely rest, relax and escape from the world. When I am giving Reiki, I can feel Sam instantly relax and his energy is always open to receiving the healing, which is wonderful. It's not often we are able to silence the "chatter" in our heads; from the feedback I receive from Sam after the sessions, Reiki has managed to do that. It leaves Sam in a very relaxed and Zen state, which is such a magical gift I am grateful to be able to give. Ralph (Sam's gorgeous sausage dog) also enjoys the experience and is often curled up nearby when the Reiki energy is flowing. Ralph is usually pretty chilled but then cannot resist joining in with a lick to my face when I am working on Sam's legs or fe et!

I genuinely believe helping Sam and being a part of Sam's journey is the reason why I qualified when I did. The timing of it all just fell into place. I am so grateful to be able to help Sam in this way, it feels like an absolute privilege to be a part of Sam's story. I continue to see Sam every other month for a good natter and then an hour of Reiki. In between our catch-ups, Sam is never far from my thoughts.

I have raised my knowledge and awareness of MND and closely followed Rob Burrow's journey and also his wife Lindsey's, to try and gain insights so I can be there for Sam and his family in whatever capacity they need. A lot of this can be difficult to read but I have found it so helpful to better understand MND, and it puts me in a more informed position to be there for Sam.

I am absolutely appalled to hear about the waiting times for much needed care, support and adaptions for people living with MND. Having to wait months or years for basic equipment or support services just isn't good enough. Things like adapting the home, providing wheelchairs, medication supplies, assigning carers and building a wet room are just a few examples of changes to the environment or services that will properly support people living with MND, and help them to enable independence and a better quality of life. This needs to change. I have also learnt that there is not enough support for the families caring for loved ones living with MND. So much more needs to be done to support these unsung heroes.

Sam's courage, strength and hope have blown me away, but then again, I wouldn't expect anything less from Sam! He was born a fighter and has always grabbed life by the balls. Sam inspired me all those years ago and continues to do so. Sam is my hero. I can only imagine it would be easy to fall into a black hole of sadness, despair, fear and I'm sure there are days like that, but Sam does not allow MND to win or to call the shots. Sam has created opportunities following his diagnosis, many of which he has now ticked off his bucket list.

What Sam has done over the last three years by raising so much awareness about this cruel illness and in turn raising a tremendous amount of money for the MND Association is just incredible. Sam is helping so many people as he navigates this uncertain journey with MND. I feel so proud to know Sam, and to call him my friend. Sam is such a wonderful human being and one I love so dearly. Thank you Sam for all the lessons you have taught me over the years and for allowing me to join you on this path – I look forward to many more catch-ups, laughs, therapy and Reiki with you.

All my love, Hannah xxx

P.S A HUGE thank you for inviting me to contribute to this book, I felt deeply moved when you asked me and I have thoroughly enjoyed reflecting on our wonderful friendship.

---

## Bev

Sam and I met way back in 1990 at primary school, then went to the same secondary school before working at Sainsbury's. It's safe to say we've spent lots of time together over the last 35 years and have watched each other grow from children into adults, before becoming parents ourselves. I have lots of lovely memories of us. Sam once recorded me on his phone secretly on New Year's Eve as I proudly sang along to Whitney Houston's "I Wanna Dance With Somebody". He's never let me live this moment down!

In 2008, we went on holiday with Jo's family to Majorca, Spain. The three of us shared a room and most days antics would occur. One late afternoon as we were getting ready to go out for dinner, Sam put on some music and on came Madonna's "Vogue". Jo and I took it upon ourselves to recreate a dance video whilst semi-dressed and Sam filmed the entire escapade on film. Do you spot a reoccurring theme here?! The same holiday I was on the phone while on the balcony, but as I have a huge fear of birds, I attempted to run inside because I spotted a bird flying towards me. I couldn't get away quick enough but slipped on the tiled flooring, right on my bum in full view of Jo and Sam. Thankfully I saw the funny side and we laughed hysterically! On another time away, Sam and I took a road trip to Great Yarmouth for a long weekend and we had a great time. A moment that I fondly remember is holding my now eldest daughter for the first time.

When Sam shared the news of his diagnosis with me I really couldn't believe it, I was devastated. I just kept asking "Why Sam?" I wanted to help him in any way I could, and ever since, we speak with each other regularly. Sam's journey with MND has had many ups and downs, I've seen the impact the illness has had on his relationships and watching the horrible disease change him physically. I can only imagine how awful it must be to be depending on others for simple things such as getting a drink or opening a door. I was proud when Sam was on TV talking about MND and raising awareness. Our relationship hasn't changed; if anything, we have become closer because of it and still talk about inappropriate things, like "Can you still have sex?"

If I could share any advice and guidance to others it would be to remind them that you are still Sam and are still here – cherish that!

---

## Kirstie

I don't quite know how to start putting into words the impact that Sam has had on my life. Sam texted me last week to say he was writing a book and would like me to add some content on our relationship together. Well, I can't begin to tell you how honoured that made me feel. Sam is one of the most significant people to have entered my life. He has made a lasting impact on the course of my life and I cannot tell you enough how grateful I am that he came to work for my company Cifas all those years ago!

Sam came to work for Cifas as a Training and Compliance Officer, fresh from Direct Line's fraud team. I was doing the same job, having blagged my way into a promotion. Our team was four-strong: our manager Christine, me, Tina and Sean and we were swamped with work. When Sam started, he hit the ground running. Sam and I worked closely together, as we did the same job. We quickly established that we both had an atrociously dirty sense of humour, a fondness for Prosecco and a shared love of the theatre. Having Sam at my side at work and now in life has taught me so much about myself and made me realise I deserved more than I was getting out of my other relationships.

My parents had been divorced since I started school and it wasn't an amicable separation. My Dad and I never really had what you could call an easy relationship. Once I got my first mobile phone, he would send me text messages of a volatile nature suggesting I was a terrible daughter, for reasons best known to him. On one occasion where my Dad had sent me a message of this nature at work, I read it with tears welling up at my desk and Sam asked what was wrong. I showed Sam the message and a look crossed his face of pure indignation. It occurred to me watching Sam that it wasn't normal to get messages like this from your Dad, the person that's meant to build you up, not tear you down. Sam gave me some advice which changed the course of my life. I needed to stand up to my Dad and tell him that I didn't deserve messages of this nature any more and wanted an apology or I was done. He said the best way to get across my point was silence after saying my piece. I had never just ignored messages from Dad, I always opted to keep the peace and apologise despite the injustice of this. I called my Dad but he didn't answer the phone. So I started writing a reply with Sam's help on how to word what I was feeling. Sam told me that, if my Dad truly valued our relationship, he would apologise. If he didn't and I gave in, then I was exposing myself to a lifetime of always being in the wrong, regardless of the truth. He has never apologised and I've felt so much peace since.

While Sam moved on from Cifas, he has always been a firm close and loyal friend. We've attended the theatre together on many occasions and I was honoured to be a guest at his wedding to James. I absolutely loved the theatrics of the day! I have never experienced a wedding that needed full guest participation in song form before and I absolutely loved it! I often get an ear worm from the song "Why does a brown cow give white milk when it only eats green grass?" as a result.

When Sam adopted his son, he exposed me to a whole new world I hadn't considered before for what some people have to do to get the family they crave. "Little Man" is an absolutely lovely little boy and a credit to both Sam and James. Through Covid, we stayed in touch and leaned on each other through the lockdowns, celebrating when we could meet up again. I got married after having to delay my wedding a year and toasted my closest friends in my bridal speech. Sam, you truly made a huge difference during that time and I will forever cherish those times we could be there for each other in spirit, if not in person.

When Sam first told me about the issues in his hand, I made a dirty joke about it. I had no idea of the significance of the pain in his hand. Sam told me about his diagnosis not long after I told him I was pregnant. It seemed so unfair to me that we were both experiencing life-changing circumstances but at opposite ends of the spectrum. We have stayed firm friends and I love that we can still talk for hours about life's ups and downs.

Sam, you are one of those special people that has made a difference in this world and I am so proud of you for not taking your diagnosis lying down. The work and awareness raising you have done for MND is nothing short of incredible. I will keep my newspaper clipping from when you helped with the MND story line in Coronation Street and show my son when he's bigger. I promise to teach my son that, when life hits you with a wild card, you hit back as hard as you can, with hope and determination for everything in your control. You are so much more than your diagnosis and I am so proud of the person you are.

Love you mate.

---

## Debbie R

My lovely husband, David, was diagnosed with MND on 8th September 2022 (the day the Queen died) and died two years, four months and nine days later in January 2025. Sam asked whether I would write some words about our experience of living with MND. I have dithered for a few months, largely because I wanted to write words that helped rather than hindered those having to cope with MND. I wanted to think, given my experience of the last few years, what I would say to myself at the point of diagnosis that would help.

### Focus on the positives

When David was first diagnosed I went in a weepy state to tell one of my best friends, who for various reasons I knew would understand. She told me to "focus on the positives". "You are going to have to adapt your house – imagine how much fun you are going to have designing your new living space". I found this more useful than anything, and certainly better than comments like "I cannot imagine what you are going through". Having said that, see my comments below in "Help your friends to know how to respond".

## A sense of humour is a wonderful thing

David had a wonderful sense of humour. I think I married him for that, and because I enjoyed his company more than anyone else I have ever met. We were extraordinarily lucky in that David never lost his voice, unlike so many others with MND, so that we could communicate easily right until the end. David continued to joke and to entertain. He could not see the point in doing anything else. He knew his time was limited, so why waste any of it.

His humour was particularly valuable in the last few days when he started to hallucinate and had times when he was delirious. In reality, we were mostly in the house alone during the last week, but as far as he was concerned there were many people with us. I asked if he minded them being there, but he was fine with it. A group of children were acting out a play in the corner (we never worked out the plot, but they got to scene five), a documentary about peasants in Eastern Europe was showing on the bedroom ceiling (but not in English and no sub-titles), and apparently people kept coming to deliver drugs (I never asked if these were medical or something else!). Oddly, it was not an unhappy time, but full of grins and jokes.

## Enjoy the technology

Technology has clearly moved on in the past few years and this made a material difference to the quality of our daily life. We loved the electric wheelchair, the slings and hoists. We learnt how to use banana boards, and green slipping sheets. The head mouse for the computer is a simple but wonderful idea. One could hate that one has to use these things, but it is worth taking satisfaction and even joy in what inventive and clever ideas people have had.

## Life is all about shit

For someone who is becoming increasingly paralysed, one of the most important things in life may really be about whether or not you have moved your bowels that morning. Accept that, and do not be embarrassed. And do not activate the self-washing toilet when no one is sitting on it. The water jet will certainly hit the ceiling and will probably soak the room outside the wet room as well.

## Disability does not make you a lesser person

Why is it that many people I meet who are physically disabled, believe they are the lesser for it. Actually the reality is that they are much more impressive. I had this conversation with David many times. I hope he finally believed me.

## Occupational therapists are the best people in the world

This is an indisputable fact. We had the privilege to work with several. MND is a particular challenge. It is not about how to deal with the current situation, but how to deal with this situation when it gets worse. Two of our OTs in particular really got this and were a joy to work with.

## Help your friends to know how to respond

For those who are not used to interacting with the disabled, nor interacting with those with a terminal condition, they often do not know what to say. I was the same before all this happened. Some friends shy away completely because they are scared of offending. What we enjoyed most were frank, open, honest discussions with friends who were curious about how we coped practically and how we were feeling. We did not find this intrusive, but rather comforting. We tried to explain that there is nothing they could say that would offend us, and that there was no problem with reminding us about our current situation, because we did not forget.

## Don't forget the socks

David's feet had a tendency to swell and were not too pretty. I was completely used to this. However, it is simple to remember the socks and make friend's lives a little bit easier, despite what I wrote in the previous section.

## Realise that, as a family, you all know that you care

In reality, this will probably happen naturally. When you know that your time is limited you have a tendency to be more open about how much you care. However, there are also stresses in day-to-day living with MND, and of course people will be irritable, and at times may say

things that are less than charitable. Don't fixate on that – see beyond it
.

## Just make the most of what you have

At times I have thought we were dealt a bad deal. However, when I really open my eyes, I see that most people have challenges in their lives, and many of them are harder than anything I have had to deal with. It seems we have high expectations of what life should give us, and when it falls short of this, we feel sorry for ourselves. Perhaps we should just lower our expectations and just make the most of whatever we have each day.

---

## Jo W.

It was 2005 that I first remember meeting you. We were both working at Churchill Insurance in the Home Claims Customer Service department in Bromley. Although we weren't on the same team at the time, I remember thinking to myself wow this guy is popular with the girls in the office ha ha... I think everyone just loved your personality and sharp sense of humour and they all wanted a gay best friend.

It was not long after that I found out we had both applied for a job on the New Claims Counter Fraud Team, and that was when our friendship began. Over the next few years, we became good friends, often spending our lunch breaks together drinking coffee, people-watching and generally taking the piss out of everything and everyone. We would always make each other laugh. We could just sit there in silence sometimes, watching the world go by. There was never that feeling of awkward silences; it just felt good being in your company. I remember a year or so later you introduced me to Jo (aka Maude) your lifelong best friend, who also came to work at Direct Line Group (formerly Churchill). The three of us became really good friends and would often hang out together inside and outside of work.

There are quite a few stand-out moments in my mind but some of the more funny memories I can recall are the Counter Fraud Oscars night in 2008 when we all got dressed up to the nines and drank and danced the night away to that Elvis impersonator. I think the video of that is lying around somewhere, lets pray that it is never to be found! Some of my fondest memories are of when we moved into our two-bed flat at 19 Thirlmere Drive in Bromley around July 2010. I still have the Gumtree ad with a list of our pro's and con's ha ha... The day we moved in, my Mum and your Dad and Becky helped us move in, in that sweltering heat. We had some real laughs at that flat, including our flat-warming party. I will always remember the night we had been out drinking in the town for someone's leaving drinks and you almost had to carry me home because I was so drunk! I kept saying to you "I want chips" and I wrongly accused you of walking me in the wrong direction for the kebab shop only to end up there as you'd promised. I even had the cheek to ask the man in the kebab shop for a few chips while we were waiting for mine! When we did eventually get home I couldn't get up the stairs to the flat and you left me at the bottom with my burger and chips, turned the lights out and went to bed! Ha ha ha... I think you had given up on me by that point and who could blame you. Another time I can recall was when the old lady across the street had caused a fire at her house and the fire brigade turned up. We were staring out the window, eyes on stalks watching the fit fireman doing their thing ha ha ha...

We would often talk about dates we were going on and some of the shitbags we had met. Then there was the time we had walked home from work, as we often did, and stopped at the corner shop so I could get a bottle of wine. When we got home we sat outside and had a cigarette; however, the bag fell over and the wine bottle smashed, you laughed your head off while I just watched my Pinot Grigio trickling down the path. I remember feeling like a child who had just had their candy taken from them ha ha ha. We spent almost two years at Thirlmere Drive and we had a blast. They will remain some of my fondest memories.

There are so many wonderful memories I will cherish, from seeing you get married to James in 2016, to adopting your beautiful son. Then not to forget days out in Greenwich Park and a trip down the Thames on the Clipper after watching the RAF Centenary fly past. "Grease" the musical in May 2022 was a particular favourite, because we got to go to the after party, courtesy of James. That was such a good night. I have the photos and video of us stuffing our faces with olives!

I will never forget the night I found out about your diagnosis. I was staying in a hotel in London when you shared the heartbreaking news in a WhatsApp message. I remember opening your message thinking, "This is a long message". Upon starting to read it I could feel tears in my eyes and a lump in my throat. I think I read it twice and in that moment, it felt like the world had stopped. I just remember thinking,

"This can't be real." I felt a whole range of emotions from sadness to guilt. I felt guilty because I remember thinking here I am enjoying my evening not knowing at that point that you had just been told you have MND. I questioned how this could be happening to one of my dearest friends and at such a young age. I will never understand why life can be so cruel sometimes.

I know our friendship has and will always continue to be close, even though we don't get to see each other as often as we would like. When we do see each other or talk on the phone it feels like nothing has changed and we can still talk for hours about absolutely anything. We have watched each other grow over the years and I want to thank you for being there and for supporting me through the good and the bad times. I not only see you as my friend but you are like a brother to me, whom I love dearly.

In the last three years you have come so far with raising awareness for MND, including your charity auction which was an amazing night and raised a substantial amount of money for such an amazing cause. You have remained so determined and strong throughout and I have learned this disease can strike anyone at any age; there is no rhyme or reason to it. You are an inspiration to all of us and your courage and strength are honourable. You have grabbed life by the balls and not let MND define who you are or what you can achieve and continue to do so

.

You will always be my dearest friend and I cherish every memory we have made and will continue to make.

---

## Jo G.

Now, I think like most people in your life, my dear Queeny, this isn't something I ever imagined doing. Having lost my blood brother in 2015, I didn't think I'd possibly be losing you, my brother from another mother, quite so soon after. Seriously, from thinking I'd be growing old with both of you by my side, to now facing the thought and realisation of neither of you being there, breaks my heart and blows my mind. How can/could neither of you want to see me old and wrinkly or insult me with those loving sarcastic comments. It's selfish to think like that, I know, but come on, I feel like my Botox and filler is wasted now...

Let's rewind 27 years; We were so young & carefree! I was taller than you at that point (Your growth spurt and impressively high quiff quickly changed that). Life hadn't corrupted us and we were closeted baby gays. We initially had different friendship circles at the start of senior school. I was very much into my sports and often found on the football pitch or sports hall. We were also in different form groups, so I do wonder if our paths would have crossed if we hadn't been sat in alphabetical order in Miss B's English class. I remember you saying years later, you felt a bit scared being sat next to me. I'm unsure if this was due to me apparently having a reputation as a flirt with the boys, or my natural resting bitch face. I won't hold either one against you, as we know both were true! I didn't really know much about you, just that the "popular" boys called you "Sailor Sam"; sly digs at your Sea Cadet hobby or possible early attempts at gay shaming. That immature nickname you were given intrigued me, as I thought, if you were gay, I'd have an ally. And yes, despite our initial protests and denial (remember Vicky, your girlfriend that no one ever met?!), we both bloody knew you were a friend of Dorothy's and I'd spend my teens hiding KD Laing CDs. Who knew this would turn into the start of a beautiful friendship marriage.

Twenty-seven years, Sam... This is why I have struggled a lot since your diagnosis and I've previously admitted to you, quite selfishly, that I buried my head in the sand. If I ignored it, it wasn't real and I wouldn't have to face anything. I know that was a proper shit thing to do and I'm sorry. I just couldn't and can't bear the thought of losing you. Having had my whole world shattered when I lost my brother, James, the thought of having to go through it again with you just made me shut down and withdraw into myself. That day you took me to Scadbury Park and told me about your diagnosis, time stood still. How on earth could something so colossally shit be happening again? I really struggled to understand why the young men, whom I love and have loved with all my heart, wanted to bloody leave me. I know I was probably being dramatic, and in hindsight, I know death is mostly out of one's control but, yeah, it honestly felt like some awful curse. It was a lot of badgering from the wife that made me realise that wallowing in self-pity was just wasting precious time with you. I know no one knows when the reaper's at the door, but at least I have some time to make more memories and engage in our gloriously bitchy and sarcastic conversations.

I have found it hard since your diagnosis; not dealing with the physical changes that you have faced, as, let's be honest, you've tried to not let this define you or stop you from living life to the fullest. The truth is, I did distance myself and it's because I know, when that awful time comes and you depart this crazy world how the family will feel. There is no beating around the bush; it's not OK, and it won't be OK for a very long time. Your parents, sibling, husband and child will not get over this. They will just slowly learn to live with you not physically being there. They will never get over that loss; they will just learn how to deal with and manage that grief over time. The heartbreak of losing a sibling. How your parents will have to cope with losing a child... I have struggled to look your family in the eye and try and pretend that things will be OK, when all I want to do is scream, "Life will never be the same". What I need you to know is, whatever happens, I am here, for you all, always. I've put my big girl's knickers on and I'm ready to fa ce this.

I have so many memories with you. You have pretty much been by my side during the pivotal moments in my life. We've seen a number of births, deaths and marriages. The tears and tantrums. Seeing you pour your heart out over cheats and liars, when in reality, they were never good enough for you in the first place. Watching you in awe, as you go through life unashamedly and unapologetically you. You have faced adversity and given it the two fingers. I could spend my lifetime chatting about all our adventures, heartbreaks, fun and happy times. And, that I will do. I will keep your memory alive. I will tell your boy, once he's older of course, of all the naughty things we used to do. I can't single out a moment, but as I sit here writing, while there are tears flowing, I have the biggest smile on my face remembering days with you. It's such a cliché, but some people don't get to experience friendships like ours and I am so proud to call you my friend and brother from another.

You haven't let this cruel disease define you and I'm so proud of all that you have achieved prior to and since the diagnosis. Raising awareness, the fundraising, continuing to live each day to the fullest. While things haven't been easy and yes, life is totally different, nothing has stood in your way. You're still Sam. Laughing, smiling and speaking your mind through all of this. Despite how shit others may be feeling, your sparkle hasn't dulled. I have seen you vulnerable and just wanted to protect you, but I know I can't wrap you in cotton wool. I've witnessed first-hand people staring at you while we've been out and making assumptions about your abilities and faculties.

You've handled this with grace, dignity and of course, a sprinkle of fierceness and sass. You may be losing functions, but you're still slaying like a boss Queen.

For now, our story isn't over, and it never really will be. Our next chapter is just beginning and we will find ways to adapt and continue our shenanigans. I love you and I'm so thankful and grateful to have you in my life.

---

## Mum

Well, where do I start?

As a mother, to be told by your son that he has a terminal illness is not something that I thought that I would ever hear. Graham, my husband, and I were aware that Sam had mentioned a problem with his wrist area in 2022, but never in a million years would have thought it would result in the diagnosis of MND.

We had heard of it, because of Stephen Hawking and Rob Burrow but, all of a sudden you are researching everything, trying to find out as much as you can and realising that happy families has turned into a nightmare for all concerned.

What did astound me is that we really are no further forward with any sort of cure. However, having seen graphs of what seems to cause it, it seems that every diagnosis is different, so there is no one-size-fits-all. So how on earth do you treat something that is so different in each individual person? If you have the genetic version you have a drug called Tofersen; if you have the sporadic version, as 98% of sufferers do, we keep being told that something may be round the corner but as the diagnoses are so different and clinical trials take so long, when will it all end?

To see your son who loved his gymnastics, went to scouts as well as Sea Cadets, and ran the London Marathon twice, slowly deteriorate in front of your eyes is so cruel; but then you realise that, with this diagnosis, there is no rhyme or reason to it.

Sam thankfully and for most of the time has a really strong mindset; don't get me wrong he can still be a pain in the bum sometimes! I take my strength from him and try and just get on with it. Of course, we all have our bad days and for me, going out in the garden or going to the local shops helps; also having family close by greatly helps even if it is for a chat over a cup of tea.

We are a small family that does not have loads of people we can call on, so we really do appreciate those that we can. We all take our time on Earth for granted, when we should be thankful for every day we are blessed with.

As, my mum would say "if you have your health, you have got everything"; being a young girl at the time, I really didn't understand what she meant but, as with most of her sayings, I do now!

Over the last three years I have had to get to grips with quite a lot: carers, wheelchairs, medication, hospital visits, feeding your son as his hands and arms no longer work, and helping him with going to the loo. Just recently, we have learnt how to use the hoist. I can't pretend otherwise; it scares me that I will mess it up, realistically, in our lifetime, who would have thought that you would need to have knowledge of such things?

Moving two households into one is not for the faint-hearted. Selling two properties to buy one property that has things that can be adapted for Sam, that six of us and the dog can move into was not without its problems. We try and get along as best we can. I try not to let things get me down too much, but try and remain as strong and positive as I can for Sam. He is dealing with enough, without his nearest and dearest falling apart. However, you do need a break every now and again. Graham and I try to get away for a two- or three-day break sometimes; it helps recharge the batteries. Carers need looking after as well.

I think that you also have to have a fairly relaxed view of how many people come through the front door; as they say "it takes a village ..."

I also have a deeper appreciation of what disabled people have to contend with when going out and about. Even, if I am out by myself I do find that I look at the thresholds of shops. Is this wheelchair friendly, is there space in the shop for the wheelchair to get around safely, do they have a working lift, and where is the closest disabled toilet? You have to plan everything in advance. This is something that I thought I would never have to think about, but it is surprising what runs through your mind.

I try and take each day as it comes. The past is gone; be in the present; the future does not exist. If I can get through the day relatively unscathed, then I consider it a good day.

---

## Becky

When I found out that Sam had been diagnosed with MND I was shocked, angry, and upset. I still think I am in shock to this day, if I am honest. Even though I see the reality of the disease every day. I remember at the time thinking (as I still do to this day) that I wish I could take it from him. It would be natural for any sibling to think that, wouldn't it? But life does not work like that. Would I handle it with the courage and dignity that Sam has? I don't know. Every day you learn something. I will be honest (and I hope Sam does not mind me saying), when he got diagnosed I immediately put him up on a pedestal... and I kept him there for a long time like he was a saint because he had this terminal illness. Over time and through very helpful counselling sessions, it has helped my process my thoughts and emotions around this. I am here to say that he is not Saint Sam!! He can still annoy m, like siblings often do! And I most certainly annoy him and I'm certainly not Saint Becky!

We made a decision as a family a couple of years ago to all move in together to be there for support. If my parents, Sam, James and I were all being honest it was maybe not the best thing to do as we are all very different people – and I say that with love in my heart. But it certainly felt the right thing to and I stand by that today. The move for me was not only about being able to support Sam, and each other but more importantly this little boy, who I call my nephew. That has been a journey in itself, helping to look after this little boy, but I Iove him to pieces even when he is answering me back! None of this has been easy and it was never going to be; there have been times when I have wanted to run. But with the support of family, friends and colleagues and using the coping mechanisms I have put in place, I manage to navigate those times.

We try to deal with things with humour in our family, the Harler way! And navigating MND has been no different. Some people may think that is strange, but for us, it helps and, if I personally didn't have that light-heartedness about an awful situation, then I would be curled up in a ball somewhere. Being able to work and be around my colleagues in the office who have been a great support, makes a difference and to some degree gives me some normality; it's a place where I feel like I can be me.

Did I think that I would ever have to care for my brother? No I didn't. You expect that, as time goes by, you will care for your parents, but never your younger brother, who has pretty much led a healthy life. The experience of being a carer has been an eye-opener. During this time, I have learnt a lot about disability and accessibility. Pushing a wheelchair, navigating the paths, I now notice every bump and crack in a pavement. Also, how some places are not accessible and sometimes, if I go into to a shop or restaurant I think, “Could Sam get his wheelchair in here?” It’s certainly not a bad thing to be more aware about accessibility, which many of us take for granted.

If I could offer any advice to carers, I would say, make sure you take time for you; your physical and mental health matter just as much as the person you are caring for. As my Mum says, we are often flying by the seat of our pants with caring. You’re always learning and we, like many others, are not professionals. Sam is lucky that he has a wonderful group of carers who come in and help him and they always make sure to ask us as individuals how we are. That simple “how are you?” makes a huge difference, as you can end up feeling a little bit lost or forgotten. That may sound a little selfish, but I know that anyone who is a carer will understand why I have said that. Ultimately that is no one’s fault; it’s just the way it can be.

Being here for Sam as carer and a sister is an honour. We often reminisce about childhood memories, and that always brings a smile to my face. We don’t always see eye to eye, but I love him and I’m proud of him in how he is navigating his journey with MND.

---

## Debbie W

Still Me: A Woman's Fight with MND

When I first noticed the slurred speech and the weakness in my arm, I thought – like many women my age – it was probably menopause. I certainly wasn't expecting a diagnosis of Motor Neurone Disease in September 2022. That day changed everything. But what hasn't changed is me – the woman who still wants to look good, raise hell, and fight back. Just in slightly different ways now.

MND has taken a lot: I can't move my arms anymore, my fingers are curling, my head drops without support and my torso is weak. Eating is a struggle, and choking is now a regular risk. But despite all that, the only thing that's really made me cry? When no one does my hair the way I like it. I was a hairdresser for 35 years – glamour isn't vanity, it's part of who I am. Losing the ability to style my hair, do my makeup or dance the night away feels like losing little pieces of myself. But I refuse to let MND take my identity too.

All my life I tried to lose weight, like many women conditioned to chase thinness. Now, I'm told I need to keep the weight on – to stay strong. The irony isn't lost on me. Neither is the fact that, of people affected by MND, once seen as an "old man's disease," 40% are women. We are the caregivers, the fixers, the ones holding families together. And when we get sick? The world doesn't quite know what to do with us. That's why I started MND Queens, a group for women like me – women who are fighting, surviving, adapting and still putting on a bit of lipstick when we can. We're a gang no one wants to join, but once you're in, you're surrounded by the fiercest, most supportive people you could ever imagine.

People often look at me and assume I have MS, not MND. There's a lack of awareness, and even more frustratingly, a lack of funding. It's not just that there's no cure – it's that it's not being prioritised. So I've made it my mission to change that. If I've still got a voice, I'm going to use it. Loudly. Publicly. And with just a touch of sparkle.

I miss the music, the dancing, and the spontaneous nights out. I miss doing my own hair. But what I've gained is a deep connection with a community that shows up, lifts each other, and laughs even on the hard days. We fight together, cry together, and celebrate even the smallest victories – because when your body is failing, your spirit has to step up.

MND is relentless. But so am I.

While I still have the strength, the voice and the platform, I'm going to keep shouting about it. Because women with MND aren't invisible. We're still here. We still care, still love, and still want to feel beautiful. And we still matter.

Debbie.

---

## Claire

Right, here we go...

Selfishly, I have struggled with Sam's diagnosis, as someone with crippling Rejection Sensitive Dysphoria (RSD) and who has a very consistent history of failed friendships since childhood. Having a best friend who will one day no longer be around is familiar territory for me, but it not being of their own volition is unfamiliar territory. However, the one thing that my husband and friends have consistently said to me is this; "Sam is still Sam..." – and they are absolutely right. The decline in Sam's mobility and varying prominence of other MND symptoms are drastically eclipsed by his highly-intelligent brain, wicked sense of humour, incredible memory and unwavering enthusiasm for an innuendo.

Sam, there are so many memories we've made that could fill up all the gigabytes on our laptops, but here are some that stand out for me – I hope they do for you too.

We first met when I joined Cifas in November 2015, and you needed assistance from someone in the office who spoke French. Obviously, with the combination of my French degree and being "the new girl in the office" I jumped at the chance to be as helpful as possible but, after I had solved the corporate query, you would over the next few weeks ask me for the French translation for a variety of words and phrases. I knew that we would get along like a house on fire when your first question was, "What's French for 'penis'...?" Our friendship blossomed, although embarrassingly I recall my manager telling me during my probation outcome meeting that, while I had passed, her last sentence was "but do leave Sam alone, you have a job to do"...!

We'd often convene in the office kitchen over a cuppa instead – perhaps I was foolishly under the illusion that my manager would perceive this as a refreshment break in lieu of just having a natter with my new best friend. On one occasion I was making myself a hot chocolate and you entered the room as I was serving (in your words) "Mount Everest-height" heaped teaspoons of cocoa powder into a mug. Your astonishment led us to giggle far too hard and we've never agreed on what quantity a "heaped teaspoon" is ever since.

Your enthusiasm for "learning" (and I use that word loosely!) the French language during the working day of course soon manifested itself in Del Boy Trotter-esque responses of "oui", "mange tout" and "petit pois" to various questions I'd ask during conversation – something you still do to this day. Naturally, when you informed me in 2024 of your imminent motorised wheelchair delivery, I couldn't possibly turn down the opportunity to purchase for you a custom registration plate of "P4T1T P015".

You mocked me following your Cifas leaving do for *years*, I remember – as I just cried the whole damn time. I've always been a sensitive soul (whereas you probably thought I was a massive twit), but I really was devastated that we'd no longer be working together given how close we'd become after just six months. Throughout that evening, you kept saying "I'm not dying!" which made me chuckle every time back then. Now, however, it is just tinged with sadness.

Since 2016, we've made a habit of venturing across London and the South East of England to sample various afternoon teas in fancy places such as Ashdown Park, Whitehall, Kensington and the Hilton Park Lane. On Sunday 28th November 2021, we went to the Shard in London for a Peter Pan-themed afternoon tea... as per, we were bringing one another up to speed on work, husbands, friendships and life in general. You then said to me that you had been experiencing slight mobility difficulties with your right hand and were awaiting further tests – I've never been well-versed in anything to do with science or medicine, so I attempted to diffuse your concern by saying "I'm sure it's nothing to worry about..." Well, don't I feel like a 42-carat plonker now.

We've been to see many theatre shows and live orchestra performances, as well as attending a closed-door Jo Malone interview and book signing, but I wouldn't even dare consider omitting mentioning when we went to see Adele in 2016 at the O2 in London. My word, that woman is sensational and then some – you do well to remind me of this (as if I need reminding!), Sam, on a *very* regular basis. That evening after the concert, I was also filled with nerves because I knew that I'd be introduced to your wonderful fiancé James, as you'd selflessly offered me your spare room for the night. Given that you'd very kindly invited my partner David and me to your wedding, when only two out of the four of us had met each other at the time, I was desperate to make a good impression. As I stepped into your Crockenhill home, which looked akin to someone's "dream home" Pinterest board, I was greeted by James and felt instantly and totally at ease. That's the first thing I noticed and felt when I met you both for the first time – albeit on different occasions – you make people feel comfortable in their own skin and in your presence, and not many people, let alone couples, have that.

One of the many commonalities that Sam and I share is ambition. As we have climbed the career ladder over the years, this has led to the undertaking and completion of various qualifications. During lockdown, I became mind-numbingly bored and decided to fill that time with doing online courses in psychology, criminology and wedding planning. Sam and I regularly joke that we will find each other the most obscure qualification going (obscure, considering our fields in fraud and financial investigations) and enrol one another on them for a laugh. For years, Sam has had his eyes on enrolling me on The Fairies & Fairy Magic Diploma, and my offering would be for him to do a course in Equestrian First Aid at Work. One day...

Furthermore, Sam is a selfless and stubborn bugger, so I'm not at all surprised that he's living life to the fullest and doing everything he can to make the world a better place.

Love you, Sammy xXx

# About Sam

SAM WAS BORN IN Sidcup, Kent, in August 1986, to parents Jayne and Graham, and he has a sister named Becky. The family spent most of Sam's childhood in Orpington, Kent. He has spent more than 20 years as an investigator, for both insurance and financial crime clients.

Sam represented the United Kingdom at the International Alliance of ALS/MND Associations in 2023 for raising awareness and fundraising, in addition to being a passionate advocate for the Motor Neurone Disease (MND) community. He has been involved with multiple campaigns for the Motor Neurone Disease Association and Marie Curie, to raise awareness for those diagnosed.

In July 2025, he won a British Insurance Award: Unsung Insurance Hero of The Year for his hard work, which was recognised by clients and colleagues, and for his personal contribution for those affected by MND. This is his debut book, and he takes great pride in this accomplishment.

He lives in Kent with his family and their playful dachshund, Ralph.

Printed in Dunstable, United Kingdom